A CONCISE DICTIONARY
OF Theological Terms

CHRISTOPHER W. MORGAN
AND ROBERT A. PETERSON

ACADEMIC
NASHVILLE, TENNESSEE

To Chelsey, with prayers that you will abound in
faith, hope, and love.
—Chris

To Noble and Blake, with prayers that you will
grow to be strong in the Lord.
—Robert

CONTENTS

Acknowledgments

We want to express gratitude to those who have impacted this project:
Shelley and Mary Pat, for your love and encouragement.

Dr. Ron Ellis, Dr. Chuck Sands, Kent Dacus, the trustees, and the administration at California Baptist University, for your strategic leadership.

Gary McDonald, SoCal Baptist Ministries, Dr. K. Milton Higgins, and the Baptist Foundation of California, for your incredible generosity.

CBU's School of Christian Ministries' leadership team, faculty, and students, for sharing life together.

Maigen Turner, for your adept assistance.

Elliott Pinegar, for your expert editing.

Dr. Kevin Hall, for your research help.

Jim Baird, Chris Thompson, Sarah Landers, Audrey Greeson, Jessi Wallace, and the whole B&H team, for your creativity, encouragement, and service to the church.

Introduction to *A Concise Dictionary of Theological Terms*

B ill grew up in a Christian home and trusted Christ at a young age. He attends a Christian college and plans to major in Christian studies. He hopes school will help him be a better husband and father, and maybe a pastor. The Old and New Testament Survey courses have shown him how little he knows about the Bible's teaching. He wants help, especially with theological words and important figures in church history.

Maria came to know Christ five years ago, all but devoured her Bible, and has grown steadily as a Christian. Recently she was asked to join the women's leadership team at her church. The plan is for her to learn to lead Bible studies. She is excited about preparing to teach women but feels inadequate. Maria says, "When I read books to learn more, I am overwhelmed by terms I do not know."

Can you identify with Bill or Maria? If so, then this book is for you.

What is the burden behind this book? By God's grace we are passionate about theology (what the Bible teaches) and the church. We are eager for believers to understand their faith so they can disciple others and reach the lost with the gospel.

What is the story behind it? We wrote a book summarizing the Bible's teachings—*Christian Theology: The Biblical Story and Our Faith*. At the end of each chapter we put key terms. Giving full definitions of those terms within it would have made the theology book clumsy. So, we wrote a separate dictionary.

What exactly is it? It is a companion to the theology book. It includes definitions for the terms at the end of the theology book's chapters and much more. We envision it as a sort of GPS to help students find their way when studying theology.

What is its audience? We wrote for any believer (in school or church) serious about understanding what the Bible teaches about God, Christ, salvation, last things, and so on. It is not a book that you read from cover to cover, but a reference book. When hearing a lecture or sermon, reading a book or a blog, or listening to a podcast, you as this book's reader would use it to look up words you don't fully understand.

What does it cover? We included entries from many sources: the Bible, theology, church history (people, movements, councils, and documents), philosophy, church practice, and more.

What is its style? We tried to make it user-friendly, clear, and easy to understand. It follows an alphabetical format including entries from "Abrahamic covenant" to "Zwinglian view of the Lord's Supper."

How do I use it? You use it to look up unfamiliar terms, such as "Bonhoeffer," "Eastern Orthodoxy," "mysticism," "new heavens and new earth," "prevenient grace," "signs of the times," and "*sola scriptura.*" We've included cross-references for easier use. At the end of many entries you'll find "*see also*" followed by related entries. Throughout the dictionary you'll also find "*see*" references with topics that point you to entries that treat those topics. For example, there appears "postmillennialism— *See* millennium," because that is where postmillennialism is treated.

Does it include common words too? Yes, because often we know something about a topic but want to know more. Examples include "hope," "assurance of salvation," "evangelicalism," "Trinity," "last days," "relativism," "Roman Catholicism," and "spiritual disciplines."

Where are the authors coming from? We are evangelical Christians who love the Lord and theology, and we want to help readers love him and it more too.

What are the dictionary's unique features? First, the dictionary is tied to *Christian Theology: The Biblical Story and Our Faith.* This volume thus covers all the key terms from that book and many more. Second, we combine words in one entry instead of separating them throughout the dictionary. This is because bringing related terms together promotes understanding. For example, instead of making seven entries for various views of the Bible's inspiration, we put them together in one longer entry, "inspiration, views," to present them in relation to one another. Third, and most important, there is another reason some entries are substantial. We wanted to show how theology is drawn from Scripture. Examples include entries on "church, pictures," "Christ's saving work," "heaven," "hell," and "Holy Spirit's works."

Does it use abbreviations? Yes, one is "c." before a date, meaning "about." For example, the church father Tertullian's dates are c. 160–220 because we don't know exactly the year he was born. Another common abbreviation is *e.g.*, which means "for example."

Allen is coleader of his church's youth group. Preparing to take his turn leading Bible studies has helped him grow in his faith. He wants to go deeper into the Bible and theology but is intimidated by the books his pastor has recommended. He would prefer that someone explain in layman's terms the Bible's teachings on topics on which he will teach—topics such as "adoption," "assurance of salvation," and the "sovereignty of God" and "free will." This dictionary is written to help people like Allen serve the Lord better. It is our prayer that God will use it to help many.

Abrahamic covenant—*See* covenant(s); new covenant.

accountability—*See* free will; Last Judgment.

active obedience of Christ—*See* Christ's obedience; Christ's saving work, biblical images.

Adonai—*See* God, names of.

adoption—God the Father's placing of believers in Christ into his family by grace. God accepts us and adopts us as his children. Before adoption we were slaves to sin and did Satan's will (Gal 4:3; 1 John 3:10). God's eternal love is the source of adoption (Eph 1:3–6), and because of his vast love, he calls us his children (1 John 3:1). The basis of adoption is Christ's death as a redemption that frees us from sin's bondage (Gal 3:13; 4:4–5). We receive adoption by faith in Christ (John 1:12; Gal 3:26). The Holy Spirit empowers us to believe that the Father has adopted us (Rom 8:15). Adoption brings wonderful results. The Spirit not only enables us to call God "Father" but also testifies to his love in our hearts (v. 16). We share a family resemblance to our heavenly Father (v. 14). He disciplines us because he loves us (Heb 12:6). Adoption is present and future, for God has made us his heirs, awaiting our inheritance of the redemption of our bodies and renewed creation (Rom 8:18–23). *See also* application of salvation.

adoptionism—*See* Christ's deity, denials; Trinity.

age to come—*See* two ages.

ages, the two—*See* two ages.

agnosticism—uncertainty as to the existence of God. *See also* apatheism; atheism; skepticism.

alien righteousness—*See* justification.

Alpha and Omega—*See* Christ's names and titles.

"already" and "not yet"—distinction between elements of predictions of last things that are "already" fulfilled and those elements that have "not yet" seen the greater fulfillment to come at the end of the age. For example, God's kingdom is present and future; he reigns in the present age (Eph 1:20–21) and will reign more fully in the age to come (Rev 19:6). Antichrists have "already" appeared: "It is the last hour. . . . Even now many antichrists have come" (1 John 2:18). But "the man of lawlessness" has not yet come, the one who "opposes and exalts himself above every so-called god" (2 Thess 2:3–4). Jesus's coming is "already," for he said that if anyone loves and obeys him, his Father and he will come and make their home with him (John 14:23). But Jesus's return is also "not yet," for he told believers, "I will come again and take you to myself, so that where I am you may be also" (John 14:3). Salvation and condemnation are realities now (John 3:17–18). But they are still future, for Jesus told what the unsaved and saved, respectively, will experience at his return: "They will go away into eternal punishment, but the righteous into eternal life" (Matt 25:46). The resurrection of the dead also exhibits both features. Jesus says that the resurrection has "already" come spiritually in the new birth (John 5:24–25) but also that it awaits fulfillment in the resurrection of the body (vv. 28–29). We live in the tension between the "already" and the "not yet." The great events of Christ's death and resurrection have occurred. Their effects have begun, but their full effects await his return. *See also* antichrist(s); eschatology; kingdom of God.

amillennialism—*See* millennium.

Anabaptists—the most important groups of the Radical Reformation. Notable leaders included Menno Simons and Jacob Hutter. In general, Anabaptists embraced believer's baptism and rejected infant baptism.

They held to the Lord's Supper as a memorial for the baptized, free will, and an early form of separation of church and state. Later, separatist forms of Anabaptism included Mennonites, Amish, and Hutterites. *See also* Calvin, John; Luther, Martin; Radical Reformation; Reformation.

analytic philosophy—an approach to philosophy that focuses on the study of language and the logical analysis of concepts instead of traditional issues. Also called linguistic philosophy, analytic philosophy has been dominant in the Western world from early in the twentieth century. Key figures include Bertrand Russell, Ludwig Wittgenstein, and G. E. Moore. *See also* epistemology; existentialism; truth; truthfulness of God.

angels—spiritual beings created holy by God in large numbers. The unfallen or elect angels have remained holy. Although angels sometimes appear in human form, they do not have physical bodies, marry, procreate, or die. In ancient times, some good angels, including Satan and demons, rebelled. These are thus the fallen angels. Angels have great but limited intelligence and strength. As creatures, angels are not to be worshipped. Good angels are God's servants who occupy four key roles. They adore God, serve as his messengers, bring God's judgment on evil human beings, and serve believers, especially by preserving them (Job 1:6; Ps 148:1–5; Isa 6:3; Col 1:16; Heb 1:6, 14; Rev 4:8). *See also* Satan and demons.

Anglicans—Protestant Christians who belong to the worldwide Church of England or Anglican Church. The Anglican Communion is an international association of churches consisting of the Church of England and churches in full communion with it. It is the third-largest church in the world, after the Roman Catholic and Eastern Orthodox Churches. The archbishop of Canterbury is its spiritual leader but has no binding authority outside of his own province. The Anglican Church is viewed as representing a middle ground between Roman Catholicism and Protestantism. The Book of Common Prayer, first compiled in 1549 and revised several times until 1662, is pivotal to Anglican worship around the globe. *See also* church, government; Eastern Orthodoxy; Episcopalians; evangelicalism; Roman Catholicism.

annihilationism—the view that lost people in hell will be destroyed after they pay the penalty for their sins. Also called conditional immortality (or conditionalism), it's the idea that God gives immortality only to those he regenerates. The lost, then, never receive the gift of immortality and cease to exist. Annihilationism is a serious error that Scripture opposes (Dan 12:2; Matt 25:41, 46; Mark 9:43–48; 2 Thess 1:9–10). Annihilationism does not fit the biblical story because, at the end of the story, the unsaved do not cease to exist but, in line with the church's historic position, endure never-ending torment in the lake of fire and are shut out forever from the new Jerusalem, the joyous dwelling place of God and his people (Rev 20:10, 14–15; 21:8; 22:14–15). *See also* hell.

Anselm of Canterbury (c. 1033/4–1109)—Benedictine monk, abbot, and theologian who originated the ontological argument for God's existence. His approach was "faith seeking understanding," using the mind to understand theology already believed. His most famous work, *Cur Deus Homo (Why God Became a Man)*, was a response for requests to discuss the incarnation. This work argues that God had to become a man to make atonement for humanity because the Savior had to be both fully divine and fully human. *See also* Christ's deity; Christ's humanity; Christ's saving work; Christ's saving work, historical views.

anthropology—in Christian theology, the study of the doctrine of human beings as created in the image of God.

anthropomorphism—the attributing of human attributes or actions to God. God is a spirit and does not have a body, but God speaks to us in human terms to help us understand him. Thus, for example, the psalmist speaks of God's power in this way: "You have a mighty arm; your hand is powerful" (Ps 89:13). David tells of God's attention to humans by ascribing to him human action: "The Lord looks down from heaven on the human race to see if there is one who is wise, one who seeks God" (Ps 14:2). *See also* anthropopathism; impassibility of God; spirituality of God.

anthropopathism—the attributing of human emotions or passions to God. Scripture speaks of God as if he had human feelings to help us understand him. This attributing of emotions to God can be observed with jealousy (Exod 20:5), anger (Num 25:3), regret (1 Sam 15:35), grief (Gen 6:6), compassion (Jer 31:20), love (Jer 31:3), and hatred (Amos 5:21). Importantly, God has divine emotions rather than human ones. Thus, God's emotions are free from the sins that frequently taint human emotions. The tension comes in acknowledging with Scripture that God is both transcendent and personal, which includes his having emotions. The occurrence of anthropopathism in Scripture does not take away from God, the holy One, who is without sin. *See also* anthropomorphism; impassibility of God; spirituality of God.

antichrist(s)/Antichrist—(1) *lowercased*: people who oppose Jesus and his incarnation and (2) *capitalized*: a final false-Christ figure. The predictions of the Antichrist, like other major features of last things, are already fulfilled in part but also will have a greater fulfillment in the future. John noted the appearance of antichrists in the first century and drew an important conclusion: "Even now many antichrists have come. By this we know that it is the last hour" (1 John 2:18). These antichrists (pl.) are people who deny that Jesus is God's Messiah and thereby deny the Father and the Son (1 John 2:22–23). They seek to deceive others with their false teaching (2 John v. 7). *The* Antichrist (sg.) is the final pseudo-messiah, who will oppose Christ and is still to come. He is "the man of lawlessness . . . the man doomed to destruction" who "opposes and exalts himself above every so-called god or object of worship" (2 Thess 2:3–4). *See also* "already" and "not yet"; signs of the times.

antinomianism—opposition to law, especially as a rule for the Christian life. Antinomians pit grace against law and claim to be governed by the former and free from the latter. In keeping with the Old Testament (Exod 20:5–6; Ps 119:98), however, Jesus and his apostles taught that although salvation is by grace and not law keeping, believers are obligated to obey the law (John 14:15, 21; 15:10; Rom 6:14–16; Gal 5:13–14; Jas 2:8, 12). Because of his emphasis on grace, Paul's opponents accused him of anti-nomianism, a charge he vehemently denied (Rom 3:8). Believers are saved and kept by God's grace, which should lead to obeying God in gratitude for his grace. God's law reflects his will; therefore, his law is good, and keeping it brings wisdom and happiness. The law condemns and drives sinners to the cross, but it also is part of God's wisdom for living according to his will—for his glory and believers' good. *See also* law, uses; legalism; sanctification; Ten Commandments.

apatheism—the view that belief in God is insignificant or irrelevant. This term was coined by Jonathan Rauch to describe a lack of interest or relaxed attitude to one's beliefs or that of others. This view entails an attitude of apathy toward any kind of question about God's existence or nonexistence or what one might believe. *See also* agnosticism; atheism; skepticism.

apocalyptic—a biblical literary genre that reveals God's hidden plans for the future in heaven and on earth. God rarely speaks in apocalyptic literature but communicates through angels and heavenly figures. Apocalyptic themes include visions and symbols of God's rule over a chaotic world, his protection of believers, and his kingdom's final victory over evil powers. Apocalyptic writing occurs in Ezekiel 1–3; Zechariah 1–6; Matthew 24; and especially in Daniel 7–12 and Revelation. *See also* hermeneutics; prophecy.

Apocrypha—books written in the intertestamental period included in the Old Testament by Roman Catholicism and Eastern Orthodoxy but never accepted by the Jews. These include 1 and 2 Esdras, Tobit, Judith, Rest of Esther, Wisdom of Solomon, Ecclesiasticus, Baruch, Letter of Jeremiah, Additions to Daniel, Prayer of Manasseh, and 1 and 2 Maccabees. *See also* canon.

Apollinarianism—*See* Christ's humanity, denials.

apologetics—formal defense of Christianity. It includes reasons for Christianity and answers objections to the faith. Appeal is made to 1 Pet 3:15–16: "[Be] ready at any time to give a defense to anyone who asks you for a reason for the hope that is in you. . . . with gentleness and respect." Christian apologetics has a long history, from the early days of the church to the more recent writings of C. S. Lewis, Ravi Zacharias, and William Lane Craig. Methods include rational arguments and appeals to fulfilled prophecy, archaeology, and changed lives. Topics include the existence of God, the reliability of Scripture, the problem of evil, and Christ's deity and resurrection. Apologetics' aim is persuasion, seeking both to strengthen believers and to remove obstacles to faith for unbelievers. *See also* gospel; Great Commission; mission.

apophatic theology—an approach to the doctrine of God that asserts it is impossible to describe God positively because human language is inadequate. Therefore, we can only say what God is *not*. Two examples are that God is not finite (infinite) and not mutable (immutable). Characteristic of Eastern Orthodoxy, apophatic (or negative) theology points to inner experience of God rather than rational articulation. *See also* Eastern Orthodoxy; mysticism.

apostasy—rejection of a faith once professed. One who commits apostasy (apostatizes) is an apostate. Christians disagree as to whether true believers can apostatize and never come back to Christ. Arminianism says this is possible, though unlikely. Calvinism says this is impossible because of God's preservation of his people for final salvation (Heb 6:4–12; 10:26–29, 39). Jesus says, "I give them eternal life, and they will never perish. No one will snatch them out of my hand" (John 10:28). Paul affirms that nothing "will be able to separate us from the love of God that is in Christ Jesus our Lord" (Rom 8:38–39). *See also* Arminianism; assurance of salvation; Calvinism.

apostle—an eyewitness of the risen Christ, commissioned by him to spread the gospel. Building upon Christ the cornerstone, God made apostles a part of the foundation of the church. In fulfillment of Jesus's words, many apostles wrote New Testament books (John 14:26; 16:13–14; Acts 1:21–22; Eph 2:19–20; 2 Pet 1:16–20). *See also* gospel; inspiration; mission.

Apostles' Creed—an early statement of Christian belief widely used by many churches. Contrary to legend, the creed was not written by the apostles. Apparently based on the old Roman Creed of the second century, the Apostles' Creed first appeared in the fourth century and reached its current form around 700. It is trinitarian in structure, with sections affirming belief in God the Father, Jesus Christ his Son, and the Holy Spirit. It also affirms belief in the church, the communion of saints, forgiveness of sins, resurrection of the dead, and eternal life. *See also* confession (3); Council of Chalcedon; Nicene Creed; Trinity.

apostolic succession—*See* church, attributes; church, government.

apostolicity of the church—*See* apostle; church, attributes.

application of salvation—God's bringing people to salvation. Distinguished from God's planning salvation before creation (predestination, election) and his accomplishing salvation in Christ in the first century (Jesus's death and resurrection). The application of salvation includes many elements, each of which helps explain salvation differently. The overarching aspect is union with Christ, the Holy Spirit's joining us spiritually to Christ so that all of his benefits become ours (Eph 2:6). Union with Christ embraces all the other aspects of the application of salvation. Regeneration is God's making alive those who are spiritually dead (1 Pet 1:3). Calling is God, through the gospel, effectively summoning to him those who were spiritually deaf and blind (Eph 4:1). Conversion is God's turning around lost people so they come to Christ. Conversion includes repentance (turning from sin) (Matt 4:17) and faith (turning to Christ) (Eph 2:8). Justification is God's declaring righteous all believers in Christ (Gal 2:16). Adoption is God's putting into his family all who trust Christ as Redeemer (Gal 4:4–5). Sanctification is both definitive and progressive. Definitive sanctification is God's setting apart sinners to holiness (1 Cor 1:2). Progressive sanctification is God's gradually building holiness into the lives of his saved people (2 Cor 7:1). Perseverance is God's keeping his people saved and their continuing to believe the gospel and live for God (Heb 12:14). Glorification is God's conforming people to the returning Christ's perfect glory (2 Thess 2:14). *See also* adoption; calling; conversion; faith; glorification; justification; perseverance; regeneration; repentance; sanctification; union with Christ.

Aquinas, Thomas (1224/25–1274)—the foremost medieval scholastic theologian, who synthesized Christian theology and Aristotelian philosophy. He wrote two masterpieces: the *Summa contra Gentiles*, to help missionaries teach and defend Christianity, and his famous *Summa theologiae*, the classical systematization of Latin theology. The Roman Catholic

Church recognizes Thomas Aquinas, whose doctrinal system and method are known as Thomism, as its leading Western philosopher and theologian. He wrote biblical commentaries, summarized five proofs for God's existence (the *quinque viae*, or "Five Ways"), and laid the philosophical foundation of transubstantiation. *See also* existence of God, arguments for the; Lord's Supper, views; Rahner, Karl; Roman Catholicism.

Arianism—*See* Christ's deity, denials.

Aristotelianism—the philosophy of Aristotle (c. 384–322 BC), a Greek philosopher during the classical period who greatly influenced Western philosophy and theology. He studied at Plato's Academy in Athens. Whereas Plato regarded things in our world as imitations of the eternal forms, Aristotle regarded the forms as attached to the things in our world, which he studied industriously. He wrote on many subjects: science, metaphysics, logic, ethics, poetry, music, rhetoric, psychology, linguistics, and politics among them. He had a profound effect on the Middle Ages, especially on Thomas Aquinas, who, using Aristotelianism, held that the image of God in humans is primarily rationality and taught the philosophy behind transubstantiation. *See also* Aquinas, Thomas; Lord's Supper, views; Platonism; Roman Catholicism.

Arminianism—theological system stemming from James Arminius that was formally presented by his followers in their protest ("The Remonstrance") at the Synod of Dort (1618–19) and later was further developed by John Wesley. The Arminians at Dort summarized their teaching in five points. (1) Conditional election: God chose people for salvation based on foreseen faith. (2) Unlimited atonement: Christ died to save all humans. (3) Total depravity: sinners are unable to save themselves (in agreement with Calvinism). (4) Resistible grace: by his grace, God gives sinners opportunity to believe or resist the gospel, and some do the latter. (5) Perseverance: at Dort, the Arminians expressed uncertainty concerning this point. Later, Wesley taught that believers can fall away from grace and be lost. *See also* Arminius, James; atonement; Calvinism; election; grace of God; perseverance; preservation; prevenient grace; total depravity; Wesley, John.

Arminius, James (1560–1609)—Dutch Reformed theologian and pastor whose views became the basis of Arminianism. As a theology professor at the University of Leiden, he came into conflict with his colleague Franciscus Gomarus over predestination. Although Arminius formerly held the Calvinist view, he came to defend a conditional election, according to which God elects to eternal life those he foreknows will believe the gospel. After Arminius's death, some of his followers signed "The Remonstrance," a theological document supporting his views. The Synod of Dort (1618–19) debated Arminius's views, condemned Arminianism, and adopted the five points of Calvinism. As a result, Arminian pastors suffered expulsion and persecution. Arminianism continues to influence many Christians, including Methodists, Nazarenes, and some Baptists. *See also* Arminianism; Calvinism; election; sovereignty of God; total depravity.

ascension of Christ—*See* Christ's saving work.

asceticism—the view that holiness is attained by denial of bodily appetites and physical pleasures, and the pursuit of rough treatment of the body. Growth in godliness is attained by downplaying the physical (eating, sex, and sleep) and accentuating the spiritual (meditation and prayer). In monasticism, asceticism was practiced by religious individuals and communities. Paul denies that asceticism produces holiness (Col 2:20–23). *See also* antinomianism; Gnosticism; law, uses; legalism; sanctification; Ten Commandments.

aseity of God—the doctrine that God has life within himself and depends on nothing else for his existence. He is the living God, who has existed forever. As Lord, he gives life to all and needs nothing (Jer 2:13; John 5:26; Acts 17:24–25). *See also* creation; eternity of God.

assurance of salvation—confidence of final salvation. Assurance is based on God's preservation, the internal witness of the Holy Spirit, and believers' perseverance. Preservation is God's saving and keeping his people saved so they do not totally and finally fall away from grace (John 10:28–30; Rom 8:29–39). God's promises to save (the gospel) and to keep (preservation) are the main basis of assurance. The Spirit's inner witness is his working in believers' hearts to convince them that they are children of God the Father, who loves them (Rom 8:16). Perseverance is believers' continuing to believe the gospel and live for God (Col 1:21–23). *See also* application of salvation; Holy Spirit's ministries; perseverance; preservation; providence.

Athanasius (c. 296–373)—Christian theologian, church father, and the chief defender of trinitarianism against Arianism. He endured five exiles because of his unwavering commitment to Christ's deity. His chief argument was that Christ must be God to be able to save sinners. Opposing Arius and several Roman emperors, Athanasius was embattled during his lifetime. Christians later esteemed his writings for their deep devotion to the Word-become-flesh and their pastoral concern. *See also* Christ's deity; Christ's incarnation; Council of Nicaea; *homoousios*; Nicene Creed; Trinity.

atheism—denial of the existence of God. *See also* agnosticism; apatheism; skepticism.

atonement—God's act of dealing with sin to bring forgiveness. Sin broke the relationship between God and human beings, but Christ's death brings restoration. Old Testament sacrifices brought forgiveness because they looked forward to Christ's once-for-all sacrifice for sin (John 1:29; Heb 9:15). Peter teaches, "Christ also suffered for sins once for all, the righteous for the unrighteous, that he might bring you to God" (1 Pet 3:18). *See also* Christ's saving work; Christ's saving work, biblical images; Christ's saving work, historical views; propitiation.

attributes of God—God's qualities that make him who he is. Clarifications are in order. First, because God is infinite, we will never (even on the new earth) know him exhaustively. Second, because God is eternal, his attributes are too. God always has been and will be loving, holy, good, and so on. Third, God is unified and indivisible. Thus, we distinguish his attributes but do not separate them. This is known as the doctrine of God's simplicity. His attributes are not parts of him. Rather, he is totally sovereign, wise, faithful, and so forth. Fourth, because God is a divine person, we focus not on the attributes but on God himself. Thus, we do not study mercy and power per se, but God as merciful and powerful. Fifth, God has revealed himself, and we can know him truly (but never exhaustively, as the first clarification states). Sixth, although attempts to categorize God's attributes are flawed, many discuss them as incommunicable (unique to him) and communicable (shared with his followers). When we label God's attributes as incommunicable and communicable, the categories overlap, but labeling reminds us of how we relate to God. Often the Bible says that we are not like God, and the incommunicable attributes highlight this. He is Creator, we are creatures; he is infinite, we are finite; and so on. The Bible also says that God created us in his image and that we must reflect him in our lives, and the communicable attributes highlight this. *See also* communicable attributes of God; eternity of God; image of God (*imago Dei*); incommunicable attributes of God; revelation.

Augsburg Confession (1530)—the principal confession of faith of the Lutheran Church, and one of the key documents of the Reformation. Written by Philip Melanchthon and approved by Martin Luther, it summarized Lutheran belief as presented to Emperor Charles V at the Diet of Augsburg. It contains twenty-one statements of belief and seven statements of Roman Catholic abuses. *See also* confession (3); Luther, Martin; Reformation; Roman Catholicism.

Augustine of Hippo (354–430)—African Christian theologian who shaped the development of Western Christianity. His principal works include *The City of God, On the Trinity,* and *Confessions.* Also known as Augustine the Great, he extolled God's grace and helped formulate the doctrine of original sin. Luther and Calvin looked to him as a father of the Reformation because of his teachings on salvation and grace. *See also* Calvin, John; grace of God; Luther, Martin; original sin; Reformation; sin; Trinity.

authority of Scripture—*See* Scripture; Scripture, attributes.

autographs—the original texts of the books of Scripture (as opposed to copies) as they came from the hands of the inspired human authors. *See also* inspiration; inspiration, views; Scripture, attributes.

Bb

banishment—*See* hell.

baptism of the Holy Spirit—the Spirit's work to unite all believers to Christ and the church. The prophet Joel and John the Baptist foretold this event (Joel 2:28–29; Matt 3:11). Luke records its fulfillment when Jesus baptized the church with the Holy Spirit on the day of Pentecost (Acts 2:1–21). Paul explains: "In one Spirit we were all baptized into one body—Jews or Greeks, slaves or free—and all were made to drink of one Spirit" (1 Cor 12:13 ESV). Paul uses the images of being baptized and drinking liquid to communicate that possession of the Spirit is essential to union with Christ. The Holy Spirit baptizes believers at conversion, incorporating them into Christ's body. The Spirit is the necessary link between believers and Christ because he unites us to Christ and one another in one body. Although some believers understand baptism of the Spirit to be a special act after regeneration evidenced by speaking in tongues, this errs on two counts. First, Paul teaches that all believers are baptized by the Spirit when they are united to Christ in salvation (Rom 8:9). Second, though all the Corinthians were baptized with the Spirit, not all of them had any one spiritual gift, including speaking in tongues (1 Cor 12:13, 30). *See also* charismatic gifts; Holy Spirit's filling; Holy Spirit's gifts; Holy Spirit's ministries; Pentecostalism; speaking in tongues.

baptism, believer's—*See* believer's baptism.

baptism, mode—the way Christian baptism is performed. The three modes are sprinkling, pouring on, or immersing (submerging) individuals being baptized. Roman Catholic, Lutheran, and Reformed churches allow baptism by all three modes but rarely practice immersion. Baptists, however, baptize only by immersion. Although churches that sprinkle (Heb 9:13) or pour (Acts 1:4–5; 2:17–18, 33) appeal to Scripture, immersion best fits biblical teaching. First, the ordinary meaning of the word "to baptize" in the New Testament seems to be "to immerse." Immersion is the unbroken practice among Greek-speaking churches, including the Greek Orthodox church. The standard Greek New Testament dictionary gives immersion as the first meaning of *baptize*. Second, examples of baptism in Scripture favor baptism by immersion. It is strongly suggested when, after being baptized, people are said to come "up out of the water" (Jesus in Mark 1:10; the Ethiopian high official in Acts 8:38–39). Indeed, there is no clear evidence in Acts for any other form of baptism. Third and most significant, immersion best depicts the essential meaning of baptism. Baptism has several meanings in the New Testament, but its most important and comprehensive meaning is union with Christ. Immersion best portrays union with Christ in his death, burial, and resurrection (Rom 6:3–5; Col 2:12). Paul teaches that believers are buried symbolically with Christ into death when they are put under the waters of baptism. They are raised with Christ when they come up out of the water. *See also* baptism, views; believer's baptism.

baptism, views—Churches differ on Christian baptism, and there are four prominent views: Roman Catholic, Lutheran, Reformed, and Baptist. Roman Catholicism baptizes infants and adults. Its view holds that baptism conveys forgiveness, new birth, and union with Christ (Catechism of the Roman Catholic Church, sec. 1213). Although the Lutheran Church–Missouri Synod (LCMS) does not hold that baptism is absolutely necessary for salvation, it says that "baptism is a miraculous means of grace" through which God creates faith in hearts, including infants', and regenerates them (LCMS website). The Reformed view holds that by baptism people, including infants, are admitted into the visible church. Baptism is a sign and seal of union with Christ, regeneration, forgiveness, and of dedication to God. It is not necessary for salvation (Westminster Confession of Faith, chap. 28). Baptists hold that baptism is the immersion of believers in water in the name of the Trinity. This obedient act symbolizes faith in Christ's death and resurrection, death to sin, and a pledge to walk in newness of life. It testifies to faith in the resurrection of the dead. It is a church ordinance, a precondition of church membership and the Lord's Supper (Baptist Faith and Message 2000, art. 7). Roman Catholicism and Lutheranism hold that baptism regenerates, but Reformed and Baptist churches do not hold this. Roman Catholic, Lutheran, and Reformed churches baptize infants and adults, while Baptists only baptize believers. Roman Catholic, Lutheran, and Reformed churches allow baptism by sprinkling, pouring, or immersion (rarely done), while Baptists baptize only by immersion. *See also* baptism, mode; believer's baptism.

baptismal regeneration—the teaching that Christian baptism brings about the forgiveness of sins and eternal life to those baptized. Some churches hold to infant (and adult) baptismal regeneration (Roman Catholicism and Lutheranism), while others hold to believers' baptismal regeneration (Churches of Christ). Proponents base baptismal regeneration on John 3:5; Acts 2:38; and Titus 3:5, while those who reject baptismal regeneration question such interpretations of these passages and stress the Bible's teaching that salvation is by grace through faith in Christ alone. *See also* baptism, mode; baptism, views; believer's baptism.

Baptist Faith and Message (BFM)—the doctrinal statement of the Southern Baptist Convention (SBC). The Convention was organized in 1845 but waited until 1925 to adopt the original BFM as a confession of faith. The BFM was revised in 1963, amended in 1998 (with a section on the family), and revised again in 2000. In keeping with Southern Baptist church government, which holds that each congregation is independent, the BFM is not binding on SBC churches. However, key leaders, faculty at SBC seminaries, and missionaries must affirm that their teaching and practice are consistent with the BFM. *See also* confession (3).

Baptists—Protestant Christians who are distinguished by their view of the believers' church, which relates to other important Baptist beliefs. Baptism is for believers by immersion as a public expression of faith. Congregational church government, the autonomy of the local church, and freedom of religion also interrelate. Baptists also hold firmly to biblical authority, salvation by grace alone through faith alone in Christ alone, and the priesthood of all believers. They are also known for their commitment to evangelism, church planting, and missions. *See also* baptism, mode; baptism, views; believer's baptism; church, government.

Barth, Karl (1886–1968)—one of the most influential Protestant theologians of the twentieth century and father of neoorthodoxy. He was the intellectual leader of the German Confessing Church, which opposed Hitler during the Second World War. A professor of systematic theology, he challenged liberalism by stressing God's transcendence over immanence and putting Christ at theology's center over liberalism's human-centered approach. He saw truth as a dialectic with conflicting ideas, such as time/eternity and the finite/infinite. For this reason neoorthodoxy was also called dialectical theology. His most famous writings were a Romans commentary and the massive and unfinished *Church Dogmatics*. Conservatives questioned his doctrine of Scripture and apparent universalism. *See also* Bonhoeffer, Dietrich; inerrancy; neoorthodoxy; omnipresence of God.

believer's baptism—the view that only believers in Christ are to be baptized. Baptists give six reasons. First, the New Testament teaches that people must believe in Christ before being baptized. People must hear the gospel and respond positively to be saved, and baptism follows this. Second, the outline of Jesus's Great Commission points to believers' baptism (Matt 28:18–20). We are to go and make disciples, whom we baptize and teach. Third, believers' baptism best fits the pattern of the book of Acts. Acts consistently presents repentance/faith/confession as a prerequisite for baptism and only records the baptism of believers (Acts 2:41; 8:12; 16:14–15; 18:8). Fourth, the connection between believers' baptism and the believers' church points to believers' baptism. In Acts 2; 16; and 18, the new believers are baptized and become a part of the local church. Fifth, there is no clear example of infant baptism in Acts, but individuals baptized are believers. Although sometimes believers' families are baptized, this presupposes faith (Acts 16:31–34). Sixth, believers' baptism best fits the meaning of baptism, for it is mainly an act of identification with Jesus's death, burial, and resurrection (Rom 6:1–4); it's also a sign of covenant relationship with him and Christians (Col 2:9–13). Only believers can identify with Jesus and enter into a covenant relationship with him. *See also* baptism, mode; baptism, views.

believers' church—*See* baptism, views; believer's baptism; church, government; church, views.

biblical criticism—using modern scientific methods to study the Bible without focusing on theology. There is a variety of methods that grew out of Enlightenment rationalism. Form criticism seeks to uncover supposed oral forms lying behind the written Scriptures. Source criticism seeks to find supposed precursors of biblical texts. Redaction criticism attempts to see how the supposed editors of the biblical books used sources to compose those books. In contrast to these methods, canonical criticism studies the Bible in its final form of a unified collection of books. *See also* Enlightenment; Kant, Immanuel; modernism; rationalism; Schleiermacher, Friedrich.

biblical theology—the study of God's unfolding story as it progresses from creation of the heavens and the earth, to the fall of our first parents into sin, to redemption in the person and work of Christ, and to his return, the final resurrection, and the new heavens and earth. This biblical story line reveals, frames, arranges, and links biblical teachings. It subdivides into Old Testament theology and New Testament theology. *See also* doctrine; systematic theology; theological method.

binding of Satan—*See* millennium.

bishops—*See* church, government.

blasphemy against the Holy Spirit—*See* unpardonable sin.

body—*See* humanity, makeup.

body of Christ—*See* church, pictures.

Bonhoeffer, Dietrich (1906–1945)—German pastor and theologian; a founding member of the Confessing Church, which opposed Hitler and Nazism. He left a safe teaching position in America to return to Germany to teach in an underground seminary. His most famous book, *The Cost of*

Discipleship (1937), shows how the Sermon on the Mount speaks to life today. Bonhoeffer famously contrasted cheap and costly grace. The former is cheap because it contains no demand for discipleship. The latter is costly because it demands that believers submit to Christ's yoke and do his will. *Life Together* (1939), written while Bonhoeffer was living in shared community amid danger, continues to speak to the church. Bonhoeffer's opposition to Hitler cost him his life. *See also* Barth, Karl; church, attributes; church, marks.

born again—*See* application of salvation; regeneration.

bride of Christ—*See* church, pictures.

Bultmann, Rudolf (1884–1976)—a major twentieth-century New Testament scholar. He initiated form criticism: seeking oral sayings in the early church that he claimed lay behind the text of the Gospels. He is best known for his theological method of demythologization. This was the attempt to strip away what he considered the husk of the mythological worldview of the New Testament to get to the kernel, its message relevant for today. For Bultmann this meant interpreting the New Testament with the aid of Martin Heidegger's existentialist philosophy. He thus rejected as myths essential Christian doctrines, including Jesus's incarnation, deity, atonement, resurrection, second coming, and the resurrection of the dead. Among his writings are *Jesus Christ and Mythology, Theology of the New Testament,* and a commentary on the Gospel of John. *See also* Christ's deity; Christ's incarnation; Christ's saving work; existentialism; Second Coming.

Cc

calling—God's summoning people to him in salvation. Often, calling is God's means of bringing people to salvation (Rom 8:30; 9:23–24; 2 Thess 2:13–14). Sometimes calling refers to the sharing and hearing of the gospel and its invitation and promises (external or gospel call). Such calling includes the gospel: we are lost and cannot rescue ourselves, Christ died and arose to rescue sinners, and we must trust him to be rescued. It includes an invitation, summoning people to trust Jesus's death and resurrection for deliverance. It includes promises: the forgiveness of sins and eternal life to believers. Many biblical texts issue the gospel call (e.g., Acts 16:31; Rom 10:9). Sometimes calling also refers to God's summoning people to him so that they trust in Christ (internal call). Examples include 2 Tim 1:9: "He has saved us and called us with a holy calling, not according to our works, but according to his own purpose and grace, which was given to us in Christ Jesus before time began" (cf. John 6:44; Rom 8:30). *See also* application of salvation; gospel.

Calvin, John (1509–1564)—French theologian and pastor in Geneva who was a leader in the Protestant Reformation. In addition to his famous systematic theology, *Institutes of the Christian Religion*, Calvin wrote commentaries on most of the books of the Bible. He founded a school that trained many students, including missionaries to France, who planted hundreds of churches. His influence continues through his example of expository preaching and the theology that bears his name (Calvinism), which stresses God's glory and sovereignty. *See also* Arminianism; Arminius, James; Calvinism; glory of God; Knox, John; preaching; Reformation; sovereignty of God; Zwingli, Ulrich.

Calvinism—theological system stemming from John Calvin's *Institutes of the Christian Religion* and the Reformed branch of the Reformation. The Synod of Dort (1618–19) further defined Calvinism in response to Arminian protests. The Synod's conclusions were later summarized as the five points of Calvinism with the acronym TULIP. *T* stands for total depravity, the view that all parts of humans are scarred by sin so that we cannot save ourselves. *U* stands for unconditional election, God's choice of people for salvation based on his own purpose and grace, not foreseen faith. *L* stands for limited atonement, which holds that Christ died to save his chosen ones from their sins. *I* stands for irresistible grace, which means that God successfully overcomes his people's opposition to the gospel. *P* stands for perseverance of the saints, which means both that God keeps believers saved and that they continue to believe the gospel. The five points of Calvinism are also called the doctrines of grace. *See also* Arminianism; Arminius, James; atonement; Calvin, John; election; grace of God; perseverance; preservation; sovereignty of God; total depravity.

canon—word meaning "measuring stick" and referring to the authoritative sixty-six books of Scripture, the thirty-nine books of the Old Testament and the twenty-seven of the New. These books function as the standard for what Christians believe and how they live. *See also* Scripture; Scripture, attributes.

Carey, William (1761–1834)—British Baptist missionary, translator, social reformer, and father of modern missions. After rejection by non-Baptist missionaries in West Bengal, India, he joined Baptist missionaries in Serampore, India. Carey founded schools and translated the Bible into many languages. He opposed sati, the practice of Indian widows' throwing themselves onto their husbands' funeral pyres. His essay, "An Enquiry into the Obligations of Christians to Use Means for the Conversion of the Heathens," sparked the founding of the Baptist Missionary Society. *See also* gospel; Great Commission; mission.

Carmichael, Amy (1867–1951)—did not allow debilitating neuralgia, which brings stabbing or burning pain, to keep her from a life-changing ministry of mercy. While listening to a message from Hudson Taylor, founder of China Inland Mission, Carmichael was called to missions. Serving with an Anglican ministry in Bangalore, India, she rescued little girls from Hindu temple prostitution and began the Dohnavur Fellowship. When too infirm to continue, Carmichael wrote many inspirational books. Her example inspired others to become missionaries. *See also* Great Commission; mission.

Catholicism—*See* Roman Catholicism.

catholicity (universality) of the church—*See* church, attributes.

cessationism—*See* charismatic gifts.

Chalcedonian Creed—*See* Council of Chalcedon.

charismatic gifts—extraordinary spiritual gifts, specifically word of wisdom, word of knowledge, healing, miracles, prophecy, distinguishing between spirits, speaking in tongues, and interpretation of tongues (1 Cor 12:8–10). Also called sign gifts because they indicate God's special presence. They characterized the early church, and the Charismatic movement of the mid-twentieth century eagerly sought them. Evangelicals are divided as to whether the charismatic gifts continue today. Continuationists hold that they do, while cessationists limit these gifts to the apostolic age—the time before the completion of the New Testament. *See also* baptism of the Holy Spirit; Holy Spirit's filling; Holy Spirit's gifts; Holy Spirit's ministries; Pentecostalism; speaking in tongues.

Chicago Statement on Biblical Inerrancy—the written product of a convention of evangelical scholars from many traditions in Chicago in 1978. The statement affirmed that Scripture is wholly truthful (without error) in its original manuscripts (autographs). It affirmed that inerrancy is the historic view of the church. In a format of affirmations and denials, the statement set forth a nuanced view of inerrancy and defended the doctrine against attacks. *See also* Henry, Carl F. H.; inerrancy; Scripture, attributes.

children of God—*See* adoption; church, pictures.

Christ as high priest—*See* Christ's saving work, biblical images.

Christ as image of God—title of the God-man Jesus Christ, who is the image of God in which Adam and Eve were first created. As the perfect image, Christ in his incarnation reveals the invisible God (Col 1:15); he does this in character, words, and deeds. When preachers proclaim the gospel of Christ, they reveal God's image (2 Cor 4:4). The incarnate Christ is a perfect example of what human beings are to be. Paul also teaches that Christ is our final goal and that God will conform believers into Christ's image. God's children will share the glory of the firstborn Son (Rom 8:29). The image bearers of Adam will be the image bearers of the second Adam when God clothes them with immortality in the resurrection (1 Cor 15:49). *See also* Christ's incarnation; gospel; image of God (*imago Dei*); resurrection; Second Coming.

Christlikeness—*See* virtues, Christian.

Christological heresies—*See* Christ's deity, denials; Christ's humanity, denials.

Christology—in Christian theology, the study of the doctrine of Christ, including his person and work.

Christophany—an Old Testament appearance of the Second Person of the Trinity. Many suggest that Isaiah saw a Christophany when he saw the Lord seated on a high throne in the temple (Isa 6:1, 5 in light of John 12:41). And some point to the appearance of the fourth man in the fiery furnace as a Christophany (Dan 3:25). These are to be distinguished from the incarnation, for in Christophanies, the Son did not become a man but only appeared temporarily. The Son's incarnation is permanent; he is the God-man forevermore. *See also* Christ's incarnation.

Christ as peacemaker—*See* Christ's saving work, biblical images; reconciliation with others.

Christ as Redeemer—*See* Christ's saving work, biblical images.

Christ, return of—*See* Second Coming.

Christ's deity—Jesus's status as God. This is an essential truth, for salvation depends on Jesus's being God (and man). Scripture proclaims that

Jesus is God in many ways. First, it identifies him with God. It applies to Old Testament passages that refer to "Yahweh" (translated in capital letters as "Lord"): Mal 3:1 in Mark 1:2, for example. The New Testament interchanges Jesus and God; God's love (Rom 8:39) is Christ's (Rom 8:35; Eph 3:19). The New Testament also calls Jesus "God" (John 1:1; 20:28; Rom 9:5; Titus 2:13; Heb 1:8; 2 Pet 1:1). Second, Jesus performs works that only God performs: creation (John 1:3; Col 1:16; Heb 1:2), providence (Col 1:16; Heb 1:3), judgment (John 5:22–23; 2 Thess 1:7–8), and salvation (Acts 4:12; Heb 9:11–12). Third, Jesus saves us in union with him (Eph 2:4–5; 1 Cor 15:22). Fourth, Jesus brings the age to come (Matt 12:28; 1 Cor 15:22–25). Fifth, Jesus receives devotion due to God alone: worship (Heb 1:6), doxology (Heb 13:20–21; 2 Pet 3:18), hymns (Eph 5:18–19), and prayer (John 14:14; Rev 22:20). *See also* Athanasius; Christ's deity, denials; Christ's exercise of attributes; Christ's states of humiliation and exaltation; Council of Nicaea; *homoousios*; Nicene Creed.

Christ's deity, denials—Doctrines that deny Christ's deity include Ebionism, adoptionism, and Arianism. Ebionism was a Jewish monotheistic denial that Christ is God. It held that at Jesus's baptism, the Christ descended upon him in the form of a dove. Near the end of Jesus's life, the Christ left him. Adoptionism (or Dynamic Monarchianism) shared similarities to Ebionism. It held that God gave the Holy Spirit to the man Jesus of Nazareth at his baptism and adopted him as his son. Thus elevated to divine sonship, Jesus performed supernatural works. Arianism arose within the church, for Arius (d. 336), for whom the heresy is named, was an elder in the church in Alexandria. Emphasizing God's uniqueness and transcendence, he denied the full deity of Christ. Instead, he held that Christ (the Word, the Son) was God's first and highest creature. He said the Father worked and works through the Word, but unlike God, the Word had a beginning. The Son is different in essence from the Father. In 325, the Council of Nicaea rightly condemned Arianism as a heresy by affirming Christ's deity. More recently, the kenosis doctrine has questioned Christ's deity. It is misleadingly named after the Greek word used to describe Jesus's "emptying" himself (Phil 2:7), where the "emptying" is not literal but metaphorical, as the next words show: "he emptied himself

by assuming the form of a servant, taking on the likeness of humanity."
The kenosis error claims that in becoming a man, Jesus relinquished certain divine attributes. The church rightly rejects this view and upholds the full deity of Christ according to Scripture. Jesus retained all of his divine qualities but used them only in obedience to his Father. *See also* Athanasius; Christ's deity; Christ's unity; Council of Nicaea; Gnosticism; *homoousios*; Nicene Creed; subordinationism.

Christ's example—*See* Christ as image of God; Christ's obedience; virtues, Christian.

Christ's exercise of attributes—the Son's use of his divine attributes while on earth. The Son of God became a genuine human being in the incarnation and retained all of his divine attributes. He did not relinquish them but gave up their independent exercise, instead using his divine powers on earth only in obedience to the Father's will. *See also* Christ's deity; Christ's humanity; Christ's incarnation; Christ's obedience.

Christ's humanity—Jesus's status as a genuine human being. This is an essential truth, for salvation depends on Jesus's authentic humanity (and deity). The Bible teaches Jesus's humanity in many ways. First, the eternal Son of God became a human being, the Son of Man (John 1:14; Heb 2:14). Second, Jesus had human needs; for example, he was tired (John 4:6), hungry (Matt 4:2; 21:18), and thirsty (19:28). Third, Jesus displayed human emotions, such as intense grief (Matt 26:38). Fourth, Jesus had human experiences, such as birth (Luke 2:6–7), growth (2:52), and death (John 19:18, 30, 33). Fifth, Jesus had a human relationship with his Father, honoring (John 8:49) and obeying him (12:49). Sixth, Jesus was "made perfect," as learning obedience through suffering perfectly qualified him experientially to redeem all who trust him as Savior (Heb 5:8–9). *See also* Christ's humanity, denials; Christ's incarnation; Christ's obedience; Christ's states of humiliation and exaltation.

Christ's humanity, denials—rejections of the biblical teaching that Christ is truly and fully human. Two such historical denials are Docetism and Apollinarianism, the former blatant and the latter more subtle. Greek philosophy held to gradations of reality, with spirit as the highest and matter less real. Ethical gradations paralleled these ontological ones so that spirit was good and matter bad. Greeks, then, thought it impossible for God to become a human being. Docetism (from the Greek *dokeō*, "I think, seem, appear") taught that Christ only appeared to be human. Apollinarianism, named after Apollinarius (fourth century AD), denied the completeness of Christ's humanity. It held that Jesus had a human body but not a human soul, "the Word" taking the place of a soul. In 381 the Council of Constantinople I condemned this heresy. While rejecting these errors, it is sometimes hard for us, who rightly affirm Christ's deity, to affirm his humanity as strongly. There are two crucial points. First, our salvation depends on Jesus's deity *and* his humanity. Jesus's humanness enabled him to die in the place of his fellow human beings to rescue them from their sins. Second, we confess mystery in the person of Christ. We cannot fully understand how he is God and man in one person. *See also* Christ's humanity; Christ's incarnation; Christ's unity; Council of Chalcedon; Gnosticism.

Christ's incarnation—the miracle of the eternal Son of God becoming a man. Scripture teaches the preexistence of the Son, for he existed before his incarnation. For all eternity the Son shared fellowship with the Father and Holy Spirit. In the incarnation he became a man: "The Word became flesh and dwelt among us" (John 1:14). His existence as a man began with his conception in Mary's womb by the Spirit. As a result, the Son, who was always God, took to himself genuine humanity and henceforth was God and man in one person. Jesus's sinlessness reminds us that sinful humanity is not normal but is a result of the fall. The union between the natures of Christ is a personal (or hypostatic) union. The basis of this union is not Jesus's humanity, which began in Bethlehem. Rather, its basis is the person of the eternal Son, who became a man of flesh while not ceasing to be God (Luke 1:31–35; Phil 2:7; Heb 2:14). *See also* Christophany; Christ's humanity; Christ's saving work; Christ's saving work, historical views; Gnosticism; Mary; subordinationism.

Christ's names and titles—designations of Christ that typically speak of his deity, humanity, identity, and mission. Representative examples include the following: He is the eternal Son of God (John 20:31), different from but equal to the Father and Holy Spirit. He is the Alpha and Omega (Rev 22:13), the First and the Last (2:8)—Old Testament titles for God. All will bow before him and confess that he is Lord (Phil 2:11), another Old Testament title used hundreds of times of God. God told both Joseph and Mary to name the baby "Jesus" (Matt 1:21; Luke 1:31), "the Lord saves," because he would save his people from their sins. He became incarnate as the Son of Man, an Old Testament title that speaks of both his deity (Dan 7:13–14) and his humanity (Ps 8:4). He alone is Savior (1 John 4:14); thus, Jesus is the only name that we must believe in to be saved (Acts 4:12). He is the Lamb of God, who dies to take away the world's sin (John 1:29). He is the Suffering Servant, who in his death takes the punishment that sinners deserve (Isa 53:5–6). He is the Good Shepherd, who lays down his life to rescue his human sheep (John 10:11, 17). He is the firstborn from the dead (Col 1:18), the first to rise never to die again, who gives life to all who trust him. Unlike unfaithful Old Testament Israel, he is the true vine, who enables all who abide in him to bear much fruit (John 15:1, 5). He is the head of his body, the church (Col 1:18), and the cornerstone (1 Pet 2:6) on which it is built. *See also* Christ's deity; Christ's humanity.

Christ's obedience—Christ's compliance with all that God required of him in his saving work, often divided between his *active* and his *passive* obedience. By Christ's active obedience is meant his lifelong obedience to his Father and the law. By Christ's passive obedience (related to his "passion" or suffering) is meant his obedience "to the point of death— even to death on a cross" (Phil 2:8 cf.; John 8:23; 12:49; 15:10; Rom 5:19). *See also* Christ's humanity; Christ's saving work; Christ's states of humiliation and exaltation.

Christ's offices—Christ's fulfillment of the three offices that God gave to Israel: prophet, priest, and king. Jesus is the great prophet of God, who brings God's final word. He did this in his earthly ministry by preaching the good news of the kingdom and calling hearers to repentance. At the Father's right hand, he sent the Spirit to empower the apostles to preach the gospel. Kings came from the tribe of Judah, of which Jesus was part, but priests came from Levi, so how could God's Messiah be both king and priest? The Lord added to the Aaronic or Levitical priesthood a superior, second priesthood. This one began with Melchizedek, king of Salem and priest of God Most High. Later, God would say about the Promised One, "You are a priest forever according to the pattern of Melchizedek" (Ps 110:4). Hebrews identifies Jesus as this priest. He, like Melchizedek, is both a king and a priest and is made a priest by God's oath. He makes atonement in his death, and in his resurrection he remains a priest, saving forever all who trust him. Jesus is the King of kings, whom the prophets foretold and the angel announced to Mary. He reigns now in heaven over his people and will reign on the new earth forever (2 Sam 7:14–17; Eph 1:20–23; Heb 1:1–2; 7:20–25; Rev 22:3). *See also* Christ's saving work.

Christ's person and work—a comprehensive way of treating who Jesus is and what he did to save sinners. The person of Christ deals with who he is, including his preexistence, incarnation, deity, humanity, sinlessness, and states of humiliation and exaltation. The work of Christ deals with what he did to rescue us, including his incarnation, sinless life, death, resurrection, ascension, session (sitting at God's right hand), intercession, and Second Coming. *See also* Christ's saving work; Christ's states of humiliation and exaltation.

Christ's saving work—Christ's effective rescue of his people, comprising nine events. Two events are prerequisites for the rest: his incarnation and sinless life. Without them there would be no cross or empty tomb. The incarnation is the eternal Son of God becoming a man (Gal 4:4–5; Heb 2:14–15). Jesus lived a life like no other—a sinless life (2 Cor 5:21; 1 Pet 3:18). Two events are the heart and soul of his saving work: his death and resurrection. The death of Christ reconciles sinners to God, redeems them from bondage to sin, pays the penalty for their sins, defeats their foes, overcomes the sin of Adam, and purifies sinners (Gal 3:13; Heb 10:14). The resurrection of Jesus as firstborn from the dead, an event insepa-rable from his death, signals his conquest of Satan and demons (1 Cor 15:21–22; 1 Pet 1:3). Five events are results of his death and resurrection. The ascension moves Christ from earth to transcendent heaven, ensur-ing that the God-man has gone to heaven as our forerunner (Acts 5:31; Heb 9:24). Christ's session is his sitting at God's right hand as prophet, priest, and King (Hebrews 1). As heavenly prophet, he gives his servants

the Spirit to spread his word. As priest, he sat down, showing the completion of his sacrifice. As King, he reigns with his Father. Christ continued
his saving work at Pentecost, pouring out the Spirit to baptize the church
into his body (Acts 1:5). Christ's work of intercession is his praying for
his people and saving forever all believers (Rom 8:34; Heb 7:25). Christ's
second coming brings final salvation, as he will raise his people, trans-
form their bodies to be like his glorious body, and usher them to the new
earth (1 Thess 1:9–10; 1 Pet 1:13). *See also* Christ's incarnation; Christ's
offices; Christ's saving work, biblical images; Christ's saving work, historical views.

Christ's saving work, biblical images—various pictures provided in
Scripture to explain the significance of Jesus's saving accomplishment.
The image of sacrifice derives from the sphere of worship. We need to be
purified because we are defiled by our sin. Christ is the Lamb of God and
great high priest, who offers himself as a sacrifice to cleanse believers
(Heb 9:12; 10:10, 14). The theme of redemption is from the domain of slavery. We need to be redeemed because we are in bondage to sin. Christ is
the Redeemer, who by his death and resurrection ransoms us from spiritual slavery into the freedom of God's children (1 Cor 6:20; 1 Pet 1:19).
The picture of reconciliation is from the field of interpersonal relations.
We need to be reconciled to God because our sin has alienated us from
him. Christ is the peacemaker, who by his death and resurrection reconciles God to us and us to God (Rom 5:10; Col 1:20–23). The result is peace
between God and us and between us and God. The image of Christus
Victor is from the world of warfare. We need to be delivered because
we have powerful spiritual enemies: sin, death, Satan, and hell. Christ is
our champion, who by his death and resurrection defeats our foes (Col
2:15; Heb 2:14–15). As a result, there is real victory in the Christian life.
The theme of re-creation is from the domain of creation. We need to be
restored because Adam's fall brought sin, death, and disorder into the
world. Christ is the second Adam, who by his obedience unto death and
resurrection reverses the effects of Adam's sin (Rom 5:18–19; 1 Cor 15:21–
22). The result is the restoration of our lost glory and dominion. The picture of legal substitution is from the field of law and features Christ our

federal head. We need to be justified because of the guilt of Adam's sin and of our own sins. Christ, the Suffering Servant, is our legal substitute, who by his death propitiates God and pays the penalty for our sins (Isa 53:5; Rom 3:25–26; Gal 3:13). As a result, God declares righteous all who trust Christ. *See also* Christ's offices; Christ's saving work; Christ's saving work, historical views; Christus Victor; propitiation.

Christ's saving work, historical views—various views throughout church history on the significance of Jesus's death. In the early church in the West, the ransom-to-Satan view held sway. This view held that Satan usurped possession of humans when Adam and Eve sinned. Christ's death paid a price to Satan to purchase the release of the prisoners (Gregory of Nyssa). In the early church in the East, deification predominated. It held that Christ in his incarnation and resurrection brought eternal life to humanity, who was otherwise mired in corruption and death (Athanasius). The satisfaction view appeared in the Middle Ages. It held that the fall offended God's honor; thus, the Son of God had to become a man so that his death of infinite value as the God-man could render satisfaction to restore God's honor (Anselm). The moral influence theory, introduced in the Middle Ages, flourished under liberalism in the nineteenth and twentieth centuries. It held that Christ died to show God's love for us to remove our fear and ignorance of God (Abelard). The Reformers Luther and Calvin, in the sixteenth century, taught both penal substitution and Christus Victor views of the atonement. The Christus Victor view holds that Christ our champion in his death and resurrection defeated our foes of sin, death, hell, and Satan. Penal substitution teaches that Christ our substitute died to pay the penalty we lawbreakers could not pay and thereby saved us from paying for our sins forever in hell. The Socinian view, emerging late in the sixteenth century, held that the man Jesus died to demonstrate perfect love for God that we must imitate to be saved (Faustus Socinus). The governmental view, set forth in the first half of the seventeenth century, viewed God as a moral governor who put Christ to death to display his hatred toward sin and maintain his moral government (Hugo Grotius). Liberalism of the nineteenth and twentieth centuries presented Christ mainly as an example and embraced the moral influence theory. By contrast, evangelicalism holds that Christ was chiefly Savior, who died in our place as our penal substitute. *See also* Christ's offices; Christ's saving work; Christ's saving work, biblical images.

Christ's states of humiliation and exaltation—two chronological phases and corresponding conditions through which the Son of God moves to accomplish redemption. The state of humiliation includes Jesus's birth, earthly life, temptations, sufferings, trials, crucifixion, death, and burial. The state of exaltation includes Jesus's resurrection, ascension, session (sitting at God's right hand), intercession, and return. In his first advent, the Son of God suffered, was tempted, was rejected, was brutalized, and died. In his second advent, he will return in power and glory to rescue believers and punish his enemies (2 Cor 8:9; Eph 1:20–21; Phil 2:6–11; Heb 9:26–28). *See also* Christ's deity; Christ's humanity; Christ's incarnation; subordinationism.

Christ's unity—Christ's status as one person with two natures. Two historical errors highlight by contrast the need to stress Christ's unity: Nestorianism and Monophysitism (Eutychianism). Nestorianism stressed the distinction between Christ's two natures to the point of dividing his person, breaking his unity. Its name is ironic because Nestorius, patriarch of Constantinople from 428 to 431, was not a Nestorian. But he did teach ambiguously concerning Christ and opened himself to attack by his opponent, Cyril of Alexandria. Monophysitism ("one nature"–ism) denies the distinction between Christ's two natures. It is also called Eutychianism, after Eutyches (c. 378–454), who incorrectly taught that the Son had two natures before the incarnation and one after, for Christ's humanity was gradually absorbed into his deity and nearly eliminated. In contrast to Nestorianism's dividing Christ into two and Monophysitism's blurring the distinction between his natures, orthodox Christianity teaches that Christ is one person with two natures joined in a personal union. Before the incarnation the Word, the Son, the Second Person of the Trinity, existed for eternity with the Father and Holy Spirit. In the incarnation the Word took to himself genuine humanity so that Christ was one person with two natures, one divine and one human. Jesus's humanity did not exist before the incarnation. Further, his humanity never existed alone but from conception was joined to the Son in Mary's womb. *See also* Christ's deity; Christ's humanity; Christ's incarnation.

Christus Victor—*See* Christ's saving work, biblical images; Christ's saving work, historical views.

church—a term (Gk., *ekklesia*) that in the New Testament refers to the people of God in various manifestations. It denotes house churches (1 Cor 16:19), citywide or metropolitan churches (Acts 8:1), those in a Roman province (provincial churches, Acts 9:31), and at times the whole church (Acts 15:22). Sometimes "church" depicts the invisible or universal church; all believers everywhere, both living and dead (Eph 1:22). The church in this sense is not identical with any one local church, denomination, or association. It is not entirely visible to human beings and refers to the sum total of believers from all places and times. In the New Testament, "church" most often refers to the local, visible church: the gathered community of God's people (Acts 14:23). The Bible's emphasis is on the church as a group of believers committed to Christ and one another, working together to glorify God and fulfill his mission. The local church is the primary locus of fellowship and worship, and is God's primary means of perpetuating evangelism, disciple-making, and ministry. Paul plants local churches, appoints leaders, and sends delegates and letters to them because they are vital to his theology and mission strategy. Under the old covenant, Israel was a mixed community of believers and unbelievers. By contrast, under the new covenant, the church is composed of only believers, as Jeremiah foresaw (Jer 31:31–34). *See also* church, attributes; church, pictures.

church, attributes—qualities essential to the church. The Nicene Creed (381) confessed belief in "one, holy, catholic, and apostolic church." From this we get the attributes of the church: unity, holiness, universality (catholicity), and apostolicity. First, unity. The church is one because believers have been united to Christ and one another. We must strive to promote this spiritual unity in the Spirit (Eph 4:3). The church's unity transcends all distinctions of social status, ethnicity, or gender (Gal 3:27–28). Adam's sin brought disunity, but God will glorify himself in the restoration of cosmic unity in Christ. Paul details church unity: "There is one body and one Spirit . . . one hope . . . one Lord, one faith, one baptism, one God and Father of all" (Eph 4:4–6). The church's unity is both a current reality and an ongoing pursuit. Second, holiness. Salvation as holiness or sanctification is initial, progressive, and final. Initial (definitive) sanctification is the Spirit's setting apart sinners unto God and holiness once and for all (1 Cor 6:11). Progressive sanctification is God's working holiness into believers' lives by turning them more and more away from sin and toward him (1 Thess 4:3–5). The Spirit uses the Word, the church, and prayer (John 17:17; 2 Thess 2:13) to do this. Final (entire) sanctification is the Holy Spirit's confirming the saints in perfect holiness at Jesus's return (Eph 5:27; 1 Thess 5:23–24). The church is holy because God dwells in believers corporately (1 Cor 3:17) and individually (6:19). Third, universality (catholicity). The church is universal, or catholic, in that it is not confined to any one location or people. Rather, it is made up of all God's people spread over the earth. This universality stems from Old Testament promises to make Abraham a blessing to all peoples (Gen 12:3) and nations (22:18). The prophets predicted that the Messiah would minister to the nations (Isa 42:1–9). The New Testament fulfills these promises when Jesus comes as the Savior of Jews and Gentiles, as the start of Jesus's Great Commission shows: "Go, therefore, and make disciples of all nations" (Matt 28:19). The apostles obey Jesus and evangelize and disciple "all nations." As a result of worldwide preaching of the gospel and church planting, the church exists around the globe. God brings into his family people "from every nation, tribe, people, and language" (Rev 7:9). Fourth, apostolicity. Contrary to Roman Catholic claims to be the only apostolic church due to apostolic succession, evangelicals hold that the church is apostolic because it is based on the apostles' teaching. God's Word and the gospel are true, so we base our beliefs, teaching, and lives on them. The apostles believe the gospel and put it at the center of their ministries (1 Cor 15:3–4). Apostolicity is so critical that preaching a different gospel brings God's curses on the preachers (Gal 1:8–9). Indeed, the Word binds all teachers to believe, guard, and pass on God's truth (2 Tim 4:1–3). Although the church is already one, holy, catholic, and apostolic, and grows in each of these aspects, only at Christ's return will he perfect his church in these attributes. *See also* church, marks; church, pictures.

church, believers'—*See* believer's baptism; church; church, government.

church, government—how the church is organized and led. Views of church government vary, but the various types have commonalities. The most common forms of church government are Roman Catholic, Episcopal, Presbyterian, and congregational. The Roman Catholic Church is a global hierarchy under the pope, the bishop of Rome. That church's final authority is found in Peter, regarded as the first pope, Christ's representative on earth. Rome claims that authority is conveyed by apostolic succession. Roman Catholicism holds to sacerdotalism, in which the pope communicates the power to forgive sins to bishops by the laying on of hands. Bishops rule over priests and deacons. Episcopal church government holds to rule by bishops, in whom the church locates its authority. Bishops may be subject to higher-ranking bishops (archbishops, metropolitans, or patriarchs). They also meet in synods. Episcopal church government is not a simple hierarchy, for some authority resides in lay councils. Presbyterian church government is representative, placing authority in a hierarchy of councils. The lowest level, called the session or consistory, is made up of elders, who govern a local church. The church's minister (teaching elder) is a member of and presides over the session. The congregation elects lay representatives (ruling elders). The session sends elders to the next level of council (presbytery or classis). The highest council is the general assembly or synod, to which each presbytery sends representatives. Congregational church government places authority in the congregation. The local congregation rules itself and elects its leaders. Churches may be led by a pastor, staff, or elders, but the congregation always has final authority. Churches may be independent or belong to a denomination. If the latter, neither the congregations nor the associations controls the other—except for the ability to leave the association. The associations are relational and financial networks of like-minded churches existing to foster church health, missions, and education. Baptists, congregationalists, and nondenominational churches often practice congregationalism. Despite the variety in forms of church government, they have common features. First, Christ is head of the church (Matt 16:18–19). He has final authority over the whole church and local congregations. Second, the Bible has authority over the church. Third, Christ exerts his authority through the church's leadership (Matt 18:15–20). Fourth, the church has two offices. The first is pastor/elder/bishop. *Pastor* denotes care and nurture with the Word (1 Pet 5:1–4), *elder* maturity (Titus 1:5–9), and *bishop* (*overseer*) leadership (1 Tim 3:1–7). A qualified pastor is a Christian of sound character who leads his family well, has a good reputation, can teach doctrine, and shows wisdom, love, humility, and self-control (vv. 1–7). Pastors shepherd and lead the church (1 Pet 5:1–5), teach the Word, oppose error (1 Tim 3:1–7), pray for the church, and set a good example. The second office is *deacon* (Phil 1:1). Their main responsibilities concern church service. Their qualifications (1 Tim 3:8–13) are similar to pastors', without the ability to teach. Fifth, spiritually gifted congregations help fulfill church ministries. Leaders teach and lead, but all members are "ministers" (Eph 4:12–16). They use their gifts to serve the Lord and the church. Sixth, church decisions should reflect the church's nature (unity, holiness, truth, and love) and mission. *See also* complementarianism and egalitarianism; Eastern Orthodoxy; Roman Catholicism.

church, local—*See* church.

church, marks—identifying features used by the sixteenth-century Protestant Reformers and their heirs to distinguish true from false churches. Reformation churches formulated three marks from Scripture to separate true churches from those of Rome and various sects. These were the pure preaching of the Word, the proper administration of the ordinances (sacraments), and the faithful exercise of church discipline. Jesus's Great Commission contains two of the marks. Discipleship includes baptism (Matt 28:19) and observance of his commands (the Word, v. 20). In Matthew, Jesus also teaches the importance of church discipline (18:15–17) and institutes the Lord's Supper (26:26–30). First, the Word. Preaching the Word means proclaiming the gospel according to biblical teaching in the power of the Spirit. This means teaching that salvation is by God's grace alone through faith alone in Christ, the only Savior, alone (Acts 4:12; Eph 2:8–9). It presents his death and resurrection as the only means of rescue from sin and hell (1 Cor 15:3–4). This mark allows Christians to unite around core biblical teachings. Second, the ordinances (sacraments). Jesus originated the two New Testament ordinances of Christian baptism and the Lord's Supper (Matt 26:26–28; 28:19–20). Both ceremonies visibly portray the gospel: baptism once (Eph 4:5) and the Lord's Supper until Jesus returns (1 Cor 11:26). Baptism and the Lord's Supper show union with Christ (Matt 28:19; Gal 3:27) and forgiveness (Acts 22:16; Matt 26:28). The church must faithfully observe these ordinances. Third, church discipline. God uses his Word, read and especially preached, to discipline his people in holiness and love. In addition, Jesus and his apostles insist that the church must discipline professing Christians who depart from core teachings (heresy) or whose lives dishonor Christ (Matt 18:15–17; 1 Cor 5:11–13; Gal 6:1–2). The goals of discipline are to glorify God, reclaim the sinner (2 Cor 2:5–8), and warn the church (1 Tim 5:19–20). Erring church members who refuse to repent risk excommunication from the Lord's Table and church membership. Churches must exercise discipline in love and gentleness (Gal 6:1–3) as a God-given means to help those who stray and to keep others from straying. *See also* church, attributes; church, pictures.

church, pictures—images that Scripture uses to describe the church. First, the church is the body of Christ. He is the head of this body, the source of its spiritual life (Col 1:18), and the church's ultimate authority (Col 2:19) whom we must obey. The Holy Spirit joins us to Christ and to one another in one body (1 Cor 12:13), Christ as the head and we as its members (v. 27). The image of the body conveys the relationship of believers, the members, not only to Christ, their head (Rom 12:6–8), but also to one another (1 Cor 12:14–27). Christ provides the stimulus for growth, but both the head and its members are active in bodily growth (Eph 4:15–16). Second, Paul portrays the church as Christ's bride, spiritually married to him. This image is full of God's grace, for Christ initiates the marriage, offering himself up in death for his bride, the church, the object of his love (Eph 5:25). Christ loves us and claims us, for Paul is concerned lest we "be seduced from a sincere and pure devotion to Christ," our husband, into spiritual adultery (2 Cor 11:2–3). Instead, as a bride submits to her loving husband, so the church submits to Christ, its loving husband (Eph 5:23–24). Third, Paul and Peter depict the church as a temple of the Spirit. Paul says that the Spirit occupies the place of the god in a Greco-Roman temple (1 Cor 3:16–17). God's presence makes a church a church, for he dwells in us individually and communally. In Christ we are the temple of the living God, worshipping the triune God (Eph 2:18). Peter says the church is a living temple, with Christ as "a living stone," alive from death and the source of spiritual life (1 Pet 2:4). Peter extends his stone imagery: as believers in Christ, we too are "living stones," drawing spiritual life from him (vv. 4–5). With these stones God builds a "spiritual house," where we serve as believer-priests to "offer spiritual sacrifices acceptable to God through Jesus Christ" (v. 5). Fourth, the church is the new humanity. Jesus is the new Adam, and God's reconciliation of Jews and Gentiles in him creates a new humanity. Christ our peace removes the hostility between Jews and Gentiles, and God makes one new humanity out of them (Eph 2:13–16). Whereas Adam and Israel failed to display God to the cosmos, Christ as the new Adam and perfect image of God succeeds. By his death and resurrection, he re-creates a people. Through union with Christ, the church is now the image of God, the one new people, called to display God to the world (Eph 2:15; 4:13, 24). The church is already the new humanity (2:14–18) but will grow into a mature humanity (4:13). The church is the firstfruits of the future new creation. Fifth, because God adopted us in Christ, the church is the family of God. Before adoption we were children of the devil and slaves of sin (Gal 4:3; 1 John 3:10). But our gracious God made us his children (1 John 3:1). God sent his Son to redeem us by dying so that the Father might adopt us (Gal 4:4–5). We are now "heirs of God and coheirs with Christ" (Rom 8:17). We will inherit God and the new heavens and new earth (1 Cor 3:21–23; Rev 21:3). Our adoption forever relates us to God and connects us to one another as God's family. We gather to inspire one another to follow Christ, which involves teaching truth, living in holiness, and serving the poor. Sixth, the church is the people of God. God made a covenant with Abraham and his offspring to be their God (Gen 17:7). He claimed the Israelites after redeeming them from Egyptian slavery (Lev 26:12). He promised in the new covenant, "I will be their God, and they will be my people" (Jer 31:33). The New Testament applies new covenant promises to the church, the people of God (Heb 8:10). God initiates in choosing, saving, keeping, and perfecting his people (John 10:14–18; Rom 8:35–39; 2 Tim 1:9–10). In the end, he will present the church in perfect holiness (Eph 5:27). It is the united people of God, not a group of individuals. Finally, we "will be his peoples, and God himself will be . . . [our] God" (Rev 21:3). *See also* church, attributes; church, marks.

clarity of Scripture—*See* Scripture; Scripture, attributes.

Comforter—*See* Holy Spirit's names and descriptions.

common grace—God's general kindness and generosity to all human beings through his providence. It is distinguished from saving grace (or special grace), which results in the salvation of believers. God gives common grace to believers and unbelievers alike (Matt 5:44–45; Acts 14:16–17). It enables unbelievers to prosper and do good and helps account for human achievement in many realms, including artistic, musical, social, and intellectual. Common grace also restrains evil and thereby provides humans with a measure of peace, making life and culture possible. *See also* application of salvation; goodness of God; grace of God; providence.

communicable attributes of God—characteristics of God that he shares with human beings. These include personality, sovereignty, wisdom, truthfulness, faithfulness, holiness, righteousness, love, grace, mercy, goodness, patience, and glory. *See also* attributes of God; incommunicable attributes of God.

communication of attributes—as noted by the church fathers, the way Scripture at times refers to the person of Christ with a title that corresponds to his divine nature while ascribing to him a quality that pertains to his human nature. Paul says that this age's rulers did not understand God's wisdom in Christ, for if they had, "they would not have crucified the Lord of glory" (1 Cor 2:8). Paul refers to Christ with the divine title "Lord of glory" while attributing to him the human quality of mortality. John calls Christ the "word of life" (a divine title) while saying that the apostles heard, saw, and touched him (1 John 1:1)—things that could not be said of God. But they were said of God incarnate, for there is a communication, a sharing, of attributes. Christ is called God, but what is said of him pertains to his being a man. In this way Scripture underlines the unity of his person, putting both natures together in a single sentence (Acts 3:15; 20:28). *See also* Christ's deity; Christ's humanity; Christ's unity.

Communion—*See* Lord's Supper; Lord's Supper, views; ordinances or sacraments.

compatibilism—the view that absolute divine sovereignty and genuine human freedom are consistent. Proponents point to Scripture that teaches both truths and admit they cannot fully explain how this is so. God has unlimited authority over nature, human life, and history (Ps 135:6; 139:16; Acts 17:26–28). Although the Creator holds human beings accountable for our actions, his creatures will never ultimately foil his sovereign plan (Ps 33:10–11; Dan 4:34–35; Eph 1:11). God created humans in his image with genuine freedom. This freedom is a part of our identity, is temporarily expressed in our fallen condition, and will be perfected in the new creation. Scripture affirms both human responsibility and divine sovereignty. For instance, Joseph's brothers sinned terribly by selling him into slavery (Gen 37:26–28). But God was in control (45:4–8), and, though we cannot fully understand, the actions that the brothers intended for evil, God overruled for good (50:20). The most striking example is Christ's crucifixion. This event was the worst crime in human history, but in it God accomplished the greatest good (Acts 2:23; 4:27–28). The evildoers did what God "had predestined to take place" (4:28). Compatibilism rejects libertarian freedom, the idea that humans are the ultimate cause of their actions. *See also* free will; incompatibilism; sovereignty of God.

complementarianism and egalitarianism—views concerning the roles of men and women in marriage and the church. Complementarians hold that men and women are equal before God but that he has assigned them different and complementary roles in marriage and the church. God designed the genders so that they complement each other in marriage, with the husband as the loving head and the wife as his submissive partner. All share equally in the service and ministries of the church with the exception of the office of elder, which is open only to men. Egalitarians hold that men and women are equal before God and that they have equal roles in marriage and the church. Husbands and wives share equal authority in the home and submit to one another. They hold that all church offices are open to both genders. *See also* church, government.

concurrence—in general, a sweeping aspect of God's providence, denied by some theologies, that asserts that God works along with his creatures, especially human beings. In particular, an aspect of the inspiration of Scripture whereby God supernaturally produces his Word by working in and with human authors. The result is the inerrant Word of God, communicated in human words. *See also* inspiration; inspiration, views; providence.

condemnation—*See* fall, the; guilt; hell; sin.

conditional immortality, conditionalism—*See* annihilationism; hell.

conditional unity—*See* humanity, makeup.

Cone, James (1938–2018)—American theologian and leading exponent of black theology and black liberation theology. Ordained in the African Methodist Episcopal Church, Cone earned a PhD in systematic theology from Northwestern University in 1965. He criticized American Christianity for promoting the white man's gospel that did not speak of blacks' struggle for liberation. In its place, Cone put a message based on black experience, history, and culture. In so doing, he believed he was following the exodus tradition, the prophets, and Jesus, who came to liberate the oppressed. Best known among his twelve books are *Black Theology and Black Power* (1969) and A *Black Theology of Liberation* (1970). *See also* liberation theology.

confession—(1) an acknowledgment and rejection of sin before God; (2) a personal declaration of faith in Christ; (3) a public declaration of faith in essential doctrines. Examples of the latter include the Apostles' Creed, the Augsburg Confession, and the Baptist Faith and Message. *See also* Apostles' Creed; Augsburg Confession; Baptist Faith and Message; repentance; Westminster Confession of Faith.

confirmation—*See* ordinances or sacraments.

congregational church government—*See* church, government.

conscience—an internal sense of moral conduct with a feeling of obligation to do right and avoid wrong. When we sin against our consciences, they convict us. *See also* obedience; sin.

consubstantiation—*See* Lord's Supper; Lord's Supper, views.

consummation—*See* heaven; hell; new heavens and new earth.

contextualization—seeking to communicate the unchanging gospel and Christian theology in language understandable to people at different times and in different cultures around the world. Paul expresses his desire to contextualize his ministry to various audiences: "I have become all things to all people, so that I may by every possible means save some" (1 Cor 9:22). Contextualization must be carefully undertaken because it involves dangers. These include failing to contextualize sufficiently and compromising the Christian message by adapting too much to the culture. *See also* gospel; Great Commission; preaching.

continuationism—*See* charismatic gifts.

conversion—turning from sin to Christ (Acts 20:21). Turning from sin is repentance, and turning to Christ is faith. So, conversion is shorthand for repentance and faith. Scripture tells of both dramatic and quiet conversions. In a dramatic one, Christ met Paul, also known as Saul, on the road to Damascus in power, knocking him down. When Saul asked, "Who are you, Lord?" Christ stunned him: "I am Jesus, the one you are persecuting" (Acts 9:5). Saul believed in Christ, calling on his name (22:16). Timothy's conversion, by contrast, was quiet. His father was an unsaved Greek, but he had a Christian mother, Eunice, and grandmother, Lois (Acts 16:1l; 2 Tim 1:5). From childhood Timothy knew God's Word that tells of salvation through faith in Christ, in whom he believed (2 Tim 3:14–15). *See also* application of salvation; faith; repentance.

cornerstone—*See* Christ's names and titles.

corruption—*See* fall, the; guilt; sin.

cosmological argument—*See* existence of God, arguments for the.

Council of Chalcedon (451)—the fourth ecumenical council of the Christian church, held at Chalcedon near Constantinople. It rejected denials of Christ's deity (Arianism), his full humanity (Apollinarianism), his unity (Nestorianism), and the distinction between his natures (Eutychianism). Its greatest achievement was producing the Chalcedonian Definition, which taught the unity of the person of Christ in two distinct natures, one human and one divine. It affirmed Jesus's full deity and genuine humanity in one person. It stated that his two natures are different but, because they are united in his person, are not to be separated. The council's Definition is regarded as the definitive statement of Christology. *See also* Christ's deity; Christ's deity, denials; Christ's humanity; Christ's humanity, denials; Christ's incarnation; Christ's unity.

Council of Constantinople I—*See* Christ's humanity, denials.

Council of Nicaea—the first ecumenical council of the Christian church, convened in 325 in Nicaea in Bithynia. It was precipitated by Arianism, a heresy that denied Christ's deity and held that he was the highest created being. The council produced the Nicene Creed, which defended Christ's deity and condemned Arianism. It asserted that the Son is eternal and is of the same nature (Gk., *homoousios*) as God the Father. *See also* Athanasius; Christ's deity; Christ's deity, denials; *homoousios*; Nicene Creed.

Council of Trent—a Roman Catholic ecumenical council that met at Trent in northern Italy in three periods between 1545 and 1563 in response to the Protestant Reformation. As the keystone of the Counter-Reformation, the Council issued condemnations of Reformation beliefs. It decreed that the Roman Catholic Church was the ultimate interpreter of the Bible and condemned Luther's teaching on salvation through faith in Christ alone. It sought to correct abuses in the Roman Catholic Church. It issued statements of the Church's teachings on Scripture and tradition, the canon, justification, salvation, purgatory, the seven sacraments, and the Mass. The Council made the Latin Vulgate the official Bible and led to the later formulation of the Tridentine (related to the Council of

Trent) Creed and the Tridentine Mass. *See also* Calvin, John; Counter-Reformation; Luther, Martin; Reformation; Roman Catholicism.

Counselor—*See* Holy Spirit's names and descriptions.

Counter-Reformation—the sixteenth- and seventeenth-century reform movement in response to the Protestant Reformation that aimed to purify and fortify the Roman Catholic Church. The Council of Trent started the Counter-Reformation. It included Robert Bellarmine's apologetic writings, the Index of Forbidden Books, political scheming, military action, exiling of Protestants, efforts to halt corruption of the clergy, heresy trials, the Inquisition, the formation of new religious orders (e.g., the Jesuits), and missionary efforts of Francis Xavier and others. *See also* apologetics; Council of Trent; Luther, Martin; Reformation; Roman Catholicism.

covenant(s)—a formal, mutually binding relationship that God makes with humans. The biblical covenants are the covenant of creation, the Noahic covenant, the Abrahamic covenant, the Mosaic or old covenant, the Davidic covenant, and the new covenant. God alone initiates a covenant. Covenants are formalized relationships that are binding on the part of God and humans. God promises to be God to his people and to fulfill other promises. In response, his people trust him and pledge faithfulness to him. In the Noahic covenant, God promised Noah and humanity that he would never again destroy all life in the world by flood (Gen 9:8–17). In the Mosaic or old covenant, God promised to make Israel his own possession and obligated them to keep his law, especially the Ten Commandments (Exodus 19–24), and God sealed the covenant with blood sacrifices. In the Davidic covenant, God gave the kingdom to David and his descendants, ultimately Christ, forever (2 Sam 7:12–16). The apex of the biblical covenants is the new covenant, predicted in the Old Testament and fulfilled in Christ, its Mediator (Heb 9:15), who ratified it with his blood (Luke 22:20). Its ultimate consummation will be in the new heavens and new earth. *See also* covenant theology; new covenant; obedience.

covenant theology—a theological system that views the Bible's story from the perspective of three covenants: the covenant of redemption, the covenant of works, and the covenant of grace. The covenant of redemption is a pact made between the persons of the Trinity to save humans through the work of the Son of God. The covenant of works is an agreement between God and Adam, promising Adam and humanity, whom Adam represented, life for obedience and death for disobedience. God makes the covenant of grace with humanity fallen in Adam and promises eternal life to all who are saved by grace through faith in the Mediator. It encompasses the biblical covenants with Noah, Abraham, Moses, David, and the new covenant, which is fulfilled in Christ. *See also* covenant(s).

creation—the eternal God's act of bringing all things into being by his powerful word, including angels, light, the earth, sky, water, vegetation, animals, and humans in his image (Gen 1:1; Rev 4:11). Creation reveals God's deity and power to everyone, always, everywhere (Ps 19:1–6; Rom 1:18–32). The Trinity inseparably performs the work of creation, namely, the Father (1 Cor 8:6), the Son (John 1:3; Col 1:16; Heb 1:2), and the Holy Spirit (Gen 1:2; Job 33:4). In creation, as in everything since, God is both transcendent and immanent. The doctrine of creation rejects the errors of naturalism, dualism, emanationism, pantheism, and deism. The main purpose of God's work of creation is his own glory (Rom 11:36). Because God's work of creation is "very good" (Gen 1:31), everything he made is intrinsically good, including physical things. Humans as God's creatures have both great gifts and limitations (Ps 8:5–6). We praise the Creator for his majestic and lovely world (Ps 19:1; 33:1–9), which points to his wisdom, power, goodness, glory, and beauty. *See also* deism; dualism; emanationism; humanity, image of God (*imago Dei*); humanity, origin; materialism; naturalism; panentheism; pantheism.

creationism—*See* humanity, origin.

creed—a summary affirmation of core Christian beliefs. Creeds are also known as statements of faith or confessions, which are usually longer. They are used in worship, initiation rites, and to combat false doctrine. Important creeds include the Apostles' Creed and the Nicene Creed. *See also* Apostles' Creed; confession (3); Nicene Creed.

curse—*See* fall, the; guilt; sin.

Dd

Davidic covenant—*See* covenant(s).

Day of Atonement—the principal day on Israel's sacrificial calendar (Leviticus 16). First, Aaron, the high priest (and his descendants after him), was only to approach the mercy seat in the most holy place after making atonement for himself and his family with a sin offering of a bull (v. 6). Aaron had to make an incense cloud to protect himself from gazing upon the Holy Presence there and dying (vv. 12–13). Aaron was to take his finger and sprinkle some of the bull's blood on the mercy seat seven times. Second, Aaron had to make a sin offering of two male goats. Aaron killed the first goat as an offering for the people's sins and sprinkled its blood on the mercy seat to make atonement for the dwelling place of God, with its altar and holy place defiled by Israel's sin. This sanctified the tabernacle (or temple) and enabled Israel to approach God in the coming year (vv. 15–16). Aaron laid both hands on the head of the live goat, confessed over it the people's sins, and sent it away into the wilderness bearing the people's sins (vv. 20–22). The symbolism plainly shows substitutionary sacrifice, for the two goats were innocent parties that served as substitutes for the sinful people. Third, Aaron had to make a burnt offering of two rams, one for himself and one for the people (vv. 24–25). Thus, the Day of Atonement answered the big problem of the Israelites' sin and impurity, which defiled both them and God's dwelling place. *See also* atonement; Christ's saving work, biblical images.

day of the Lord—a future day of judgment that the New Testament links to Christ's second coming. The Old Testament warns that "the day of the LORD is near and will come as devastation from the Almighty" (Joel 1:15).

It is the day of God's judgment on his people Israel (Zeph 1:4–13), but not only so, "for the day of the LORD is . . . against all the nations" (Obad 1:15). The Old Testament ends with God's promise that the day is still future: "Look, I am going to send you the prophet Elijah before the great and terrible day of the LORD comes" (Mal 4:5). The New Testament still speaks of the day of the Lord as a day of judgment (1 Thess 5:2–4; 2 Pet 3:10). But the Old Testament day of the Lord has become "the day of our Lord Jesus Christ" (1 Cor 1:8), the day of his return. The day of the Lord Jesus is a day of judgment *and* salvation (1 Cor 1:8; 2 Cor 1:14). *See also* hell; Last Judgment; Second Coming.

deacons—*See* church, government.

death—the penalty for sin. Death is unnatural and is a consequence of the fall of Adam and Eve into sin (Gen 2:17; 3:19). Death signifies separation in all its aspects. Spiritual death is separation from God, as is evident when Adam and Eve hid from God after sinning (v. 8). Although unsaved people are physically alive, they are "dead in . . . trespasses and sins," that is, separated from the life of God (Eph 2:1, 5). Physical death is separation of body and soul (Luke 16:22–23; 23:46; 2 Cor 5:6, 8). The second death is eternal separation from God in hell (Rev 20:14; 21:8). Christ, at his return, will vanquish all foes, including death (1 Cor 15:25–26). Although the complete results of his victory are still future, Christ in his death and resurrection has already conquered death. When God gives us the new birth, he makes us alive spiritually (Eph 2:5). And when God raises us from the dead to eternal life in immortal bodies, he will overcome spiritual and physical death forever. *See also* fall, the; guilt; hell; Last Judgment; regeneration; Second Coming; sin.

death of Christ—*See* Christ's saving work; Christ's saving work, biblical images; Christ's saving work, historical views.

deification—*See* Christ's saving work, historical views; Eastern Orthodoxy.

deism—an eighteenth-century philosophy that held that the Creator built into the world the ability to run on its own without his involvement. Thus, deism removed God from the world. The doctrine of providence refutes deism because God not only made the world but continues to sustain and guide it. *See also* creation; omnipresence of God; providence.

deistic evolution—*See* humanity, origin.

deity of the Holy Spirit—*See* Holy Spirit's deity.

demon possession—*See* exorcism.

demons—*See* Satan and demons.

demythologization—*See* Bultmann, Rudolf.

denomination—a distinct religious organization within Christianity, consisting of local churches identified by name, government, leadership, and some beliefs. *See also* Anglicans; Baptists; Eastern Orthodoxy; Lutherans; Methodists; Pentecostalism; Presbyterians; Roman Catholicism.

depravity, total—*See* total depravity.

descent into hell (*Hades*)—the view that between his death and resurrection Christ visited the abode of the dead in the netherworld. Support comes from the statement "[Christ] descended into hell" in later versions of the Apostles' Creed and from statements made by church fathers. There are good reasons to reject the descent into hell, however. Earlier versions of the Apostles' Creed lack the statement, and even after its insertion the phrase could be translated "he descended into the grave." More telling, the view lacks clear biblical evidence, although proponents appeal to Eph 4:9–10 and 1 Pet 3:19–20. All things considered, it is better to abandon the notion of a literal descent and to follow Calvin and the Heidelberg Catechism in understanding the descent as speaking figuratively of Christ's suffering the pains of hell on the cross. *See also* Apostles' Creed; Christ's saving work; Christ's saving work, biblical images.

destinies, eternal—*See* heaven; hell; new heavens and new earth.

destruction—*See* hell; sin.

devil—*See* Satan and demons.

dialectical theology—*See* Barth, Karl; neoorthodoxy.

dichotomy—*See* humanity, makeup.

dictation theory of inspiration—*See* inspiration, views.

disciple—a follower of Jesus Christ. This term originally referred to the Twelve whom Jesus chose to be with him and to learn from him (Matt 10:1) but was later applied to all who identified with him (Matt 28:19; Acts 6:1–2, 7). *See also* Great Commission; spiritual disciplines; spirituality.

discipleship—*See* Great Commission; spiritual disciplines; spirituality.

discipline—*See* adoption; church, marks.

dispensationalism—an evangelical system of theology that divides Scripture into different eras or dispensations in which God relates to people in different ways. The *Scofield Reference Bible* popularized dispensationalism in the early twentieth century and divided Scripture into seven dispensations: innocence, conscience, human government, promise, the law, grace or the church, and a future millennial kingdom with Christ reigning over Israel. Emphases included the literal interpretation of Scripture—especially prophecy, distinctions between national Israel and the church and between law and grace, and a pretribulation rapture of the church before the seven-year tribulation and Jewish millennium. Progressive dispensationalism softens the Israel/church distinction. *See also* millennium; Second Coming; tribulation.

dispensational premillennialism—*See* millennium.

Docetism—*See* Christ's humanity; Christ's humanity, denials.

doctrine—a summary of biblical teaching on a particular theme. Jesus's teaching was from his Father (John 7:16) and astonished the crowds (Matt 22:33). After Paul affirms that God is the Author of Scripture, he says that Scripture "is profitable for teaching" or doctrine (2 Tim 3:16). Scripture is concerned with the promotion of sound doctrine and opposition to false doctrine (1 Tim 1:3; 6:3). Pastors are to adhere "to the pattern of sound teaching" (2 Tim 1:13) and only preach "things consistent with sound teaching" (Titus 2:1). There are those who teach false doctrine and contradict sound teaching (1 Tim 6:3; Eph 4:14). Therefore, elders must hold fast to the gospel so they can both "encourage with sound teaching and . . . refute those who contradict it" (Titus 1:9). Examples include the doctrines of the Trinity, Christ, the church, and last things. *See also* heresy; systematic theology; theology.

Dort, Synod of—*See* Arminianism; Arminius, James; Calvinism.

down payment—*See* Holy Spirit's names and descriptions.

dualism—the philosophical view that reality or an aspect of it is composed of two substances or principles. There are different types of dualism, two of which are pertinent here. Ontological dualism is the belief that there are two eternal principles of good and evil (e.g., in Manichaeism). Scripture opposes this view by teaching that the eternal almighty Creator is the ultimate reality. Evil is not a competing eternal principle with God but an aberration of God's good creation. Mind/body dualism views mind and matter (body) as separate and holds that mental activity is, in some respects, not physical (e.g., in Descartes). *See also* creation; eternity of God; fall, the; humanity, makeup; humanity, states; materialism; monism; naturalism; sin.

Dynamic Monarchianism—*See* Christ's deity, denials; Trinity.

dynamic theory of inspiration—*See* inspiration, views.

Ee

Eareckson Tada, Joni (1949–)—against great odds began a world-wide ministry to the disabled. As a teenager, she had a diving accident that paralyzed her from the shoulders down. In 1976 she wrote the best-selling biography: *Joni: The Unforgettable Story of a Young Woman's Struggle against Quadriplegia and Depression.* In 1979 she founded Joni and Friends, a Christian ministry to the disabled that has helped many around the world. Eareckson Tada was a plenary speaker at the Second International Congress on World Evangelism in Manila (1989), helped form a theology of disability, and contributed to the Americans with Disabilities Act (1990). *See also* Great Commission; mission.

Eastern Orthodoxy—the church of the seven councils and one of the three main branches of Christianity, along with Roman Catholicism and Protestantism. Eastern Orthodoxy broke with the Roman Catholic Church, largely over the pope's authority, in the Great Schism of 1054. It is composed of self-governing territorial churches (e.g., Greek Orthodox Church, Russian Orthodox Church). It is based on Holy Tradition, which it traces back to Jesus and the apostles. It holds to apophatic theology: God is beyond rational understanding and can be understood only in statements of what he is not. Orthodoxy believes that the Spirit proceeds from the Father only, not the Son. Orthodoxy regards salvation as a process of deification, in which Orthodox believers participate in God's nature (2 Pet 1:4). *See also* apophatic theology; church, government; evangelicalism; Roman Catholicism; theology, sources.

Ebionism—*See* Christ's deity, denials.

ecclesiology—in Christian theology, the study of the doctrine of the church, including its nature, attributes, marks, structure, ordinances, and purposes.

economic Trinity—*See* Trinity; Trinity, ontological/economic.

ecumenism—the endeavor to generate worldwide unity among churches, by cooperation or organic union. Ecumenism acknowledges schisms in church history, including the Great Schism of 1054 between Roman Catholic and Orthodox churches and the Reformation of the sixteenth century between Protestant and Roman Catholic churches. Early twentieth-century missions conferences, bringing together Christians for world evangelism, provided momentum for the ecumenical movement. Positively, the movement underscores the need for believers to seek unity without forfeiting doctrinal integrity. Negatively, it underscores theological and evangelistic negligence and left-leaning political thought. *See also* Eastern Orthodoxy; evangelicalism; neoorthodoxy; Reformation; Roman Catholicism.

Edwards, Jonathan (1703–1758)—American Congregationalist pastor, revivalist preacher, theologian, and philosopher who played a vital role in the First Great Awakening. One of America's leading theologians, he authored many books, including *The End for Which God Created the World*; *The Life of David Brainerd*, which inspired thousands of missionaries in the nineteenth century; and *Religious Affections*, which many Christians still read today. Although most known for his sermon "Sinners in the Hands of an Angry God," Edwards was a theologian who preached and wrote extensively on many theological themes, particularly the glory of God, the Trinity, God's sovereignty and human freedom, original sin, justification, heaven and hell, revival happiness, and love. *See also* Great Commission; mission.

effectual call—*See* calling.

ekklesia—*See* church.

elders—*See* church, government.

election—God's choosing people for salvation. He is its Author, for he chose and predestined believers (Eph 1:4–5). In love God chose Israel out of all the nations (Deut 7:6–8; 10:14–15). He also chose the Messiah (Luke 9:35; 1 Pet 1:20). Jesus, the Chosen One, chose his disciples to belong to him instead of to the world (John 15:16, 19). If we received what our sins deserved, we would be condemned. But God in grace chose us, who did not seek him, and gave us what we did not deserve: eternal life (Acts 13:48; Rom 3:9–20). Our salvation is based on God's mercy and initiative (Rom 9:15–16). Election is based on God's foreknowledge (Rom 8:29; 1 Pet 1:1–2). New Testament language concerning the chosen is mostly plural. It also teaches individual election (Acts 13:48; Rom 9:15), so election is both collective and personal. Paul combines election and union with Christ (Eph 1:4; 2 Tim 1:9). God chose us for salvation before creation and also planned the means to save us—to send his Son to die, rise, and send the Spirit to join believers to Christ in salvation. God chose us for salvation before creation, locating election in God, not us (Eph 1:4; 2 Tim 1:9). Paul traces our election to God's love, grace, and mercy, and also to his purpose or will (Rom 9:15–16; Eph 1:4–6, 11). Paul gives the negative and positive reasons for election: it is based not on human desire or endeavor but on a merciful God (Rom 9:16). In sum, election has its basis in God's "own purpose and grace" (2 Tim 1:9). Election has purposes: to make us holy (Eph 1:4), to boost assurance (John 10:27–29), to conform us to Christ's image (Rom 8:29–30), to foster missions (9:1–5; 10:13–17), and to elicit praise (Eph 1:3, 6, 12, 14), humility (Rom 9:15–16), renewed service (Acts 18:9–10), and passionate evangelism (Rom 9:1–3; 10:1–17). The ultimate end of election is not our salvation but God's glory (Eph 1:6, 12, 14). Election upholds human responsibility for faith and the necessity of evangelism and missions. *See also* compatibilism; foreknowledge; free will; incompatibilism; mission; sovereignty of God.

elements (Communion)—*See* Lord's Supper, views.

Elohim—*See* God, names of.

emanationism—the belief that the world is an emanation or extension of God himself. Creation, therefore, would be an overflow of God's being.

To the contrary, Scripture teaches that the Creator is distinct from his creation. He alone existed from eternity and created the world, and it remains distinct from him. *See also* creation; deism; dualism; omnipresence of God; panentheism; pantheism.

empiricism—the philosophy that all knowledge is gained through sense experience rather than through reason, authority, or intuition. It arose with the science of Francis Bacon (1561–1626), was developed by John Locke (1632–1704), and reached its zenith with David Hume (1711–1776). Hume's agnosticism concerning the knowledge of things outside of us resulted in his skepticism and naturalism. *See also* agnosticism; epistemology; naturalism; rationalism; skepticism.

empowering of the Spirit—*See* Holy Spirit's ministries.

Enlightenment, the—an eighteenth-century European movement in philosophy, science, and politics that spurned external authorities, including tradition, Scripture, the church, the monarchy, and elevated reason. For this reason it is also called the Age of Reason. Its key figures included David Hume, Immanuel Kant, Voltaire, Jean-Jacques Rousseau, Goethe, and Adam Smith. Exalting liberty, progress, and the separation of church and state, it spawned the scientific method, political revolutions, and the rise of modernity. *See also* Kant, Immanuel; liberalism; modernism; rationalism; Schleiermacher, Friedrich.

Episcopal church government—*See* church, government.

Episcopalians—Protestant Christians who belong to the Episcopal Church, an American member of the worldwide Anglican Church. It began when it separated from the Church of England after the Revolutionary War. It is called "Episcopal" after the Greek word for "bishop" or "overseer" because it appoints bishops for regional oversight of the churches. Its Book of Common Prayer is central to all Anglican worship. It holds to baptismal regeneration and the Holy Eucharist as its principal acts of worship. The Episcopal Church has moved in a liberal direction since the 1960s and today promotes same-sex marriage and the ordination of LGBT people. It has declined in membership and attendance since 2000. *See also* Anglicans; church, government; Eastern Orthodoxy; evangelicalism.

epistemology—the philosophical study of human knowledge, including its nature, origin, and limits. Also called the theory of knowledge. Epistemology has a long history in Western philosophy, beginning with the ancient Greeks and continuing to today. It has taken one of two paths: rationalism (which seeks knowledge through reason) and empiricism (which seeks knowledge through the senses). It seeks to answer questions, such as "What does it mean to know something?" and "How do we know that we know?" It is one of the four main branches of philosophy. *See also* ethics; logic; metaphysics.

Erasmus (c. 1466–1536)—a brilliant linguistic scholar and the principal figure of the early northern Renaissance. His *In Praise of Folly* poked satirically at the abuses of society and the church. He promoted classical knowledge to improve morality and peace. His edition of the Greek New Testament (1516) helped spark the Reformation because it enabled people to challenge Roman Catholic doctrines in the light of the original Greek. After Luther's Ninety-Five Theses ignited the Reformation, Erasmus found himself in debate over human nature, sin, and free will. Although he supported Luther's ideals, he rejected what he considered Luther's radicalism and remained a Catholic. He opposed Luther's theology in *The Freedom of the Will* (1523). *See also* Luther, Martin; Reformation.

eschatology—in Christian theology, the study of the doctrine of last things, both of individuals and of the world. Individual eschatology concerns death, the intermediate state, the resurrection, and eternal destiny. General eschatology concerns the return of Christ, the resurrection of the dead, the Last Judgment, and the eternal destinies of eternal life on the new earth or eternal punishment in hell. *See also* "already" and "not yet"; death; eternal life; heaven; hell; intermediate state; Last Judgment; millennium; new earth; resurrection; Second Coming.

estrangement—*See* fall, the; hell; sin.

eternal generation—a phrase that expresses the eternal relationship between the First and Second Persons of the Trinity. God the Father eternally "generates" or "begets" the Son. This means that the Son's identity is defined eternally by his relationship with the Father. Likewise, the Father's identity is defined eternally by his relationship with the Son. Eternal generation expresses that the Son is one with the Father in deity and glory and yet distinct from him. Eternal generation does not mean that the Father created the Son but that the Son has an eternal relationship with the Father. This doctrine is taught in the Nicene Creed, the Belgic Confession (articles X and XI), and the Westminster Confession of Faith (II.3). *See also* Christ's deity; eternal procession; Nicene Creed; Trinity.

eternal life—the quality and duration of a believer's existence. As a quality of life, eternal life begins the moment a person trusts Jesus as Lord and Savior. It is knowing God through Christ (John 17:3). Although all human beings will exist forever, not all will enjoy eternal life forever. Scripture calls suffering in hell forever not "life" but "death" (Rev 2:11; 20:6, 14; 21:8). In contrast, eternal life in its ultimate sense is knowing and enjoying God forever as resurrected persons on the new earth (Matt 25:46). *See also* "already" and "not yet"; heaven; hell; new heavens and new earth; regeneration; resurrection.

eternal procession—a phrase that expresses the eternal relationship between the Third and the First and Second Persons of the Trinity. God the Holy Spirit eternally proceeds from God the Father and God the Son. This means that the Spirit's identity is defined eternally by his relationship with the Father and the Son. Likewise, the Father's and Son's identities are defined eternally by their relationship with the Spirit. Eternal procession does not mean that the Father and Son created the Spirit, but expresses the Spirit's eternal relationship with them both. The Spirit is fully God, as are the Father and the Son; yet God is three in one, the Trinity. *See also* eternal generation; Holy Spirit's deity; Nicene Creed; Trinity.

eternal punishment—*See* hell.

eternal security—*See* assurance of salvation; preservation.

eternal state—*See* heaven; hell; humanity, states; new heavens and new earth.

eternity of God—the attribute of the living and true God as the Lord of time. As its Creator, he stands outside of time, not being trapped within it but, rather, controlling it. He also enters into time in order to relate to us, who are time-bound. We face the future with confidence in the eternal God, who both inhabits eternity and dwells with us, his people (Ps 90:4; Isa 40:28–30; Rom 16:26; 1 Tim 1:17). *See also* creation; Holy Spirit's indwelling.

ethics—also called moral philosophy, the discipline concerned with what is morally right and wrong and what it means to live the good life. Term also applies to any system of moral principles. Ethical systems emphasize either duty (deontological ethics), consequences (teleological ethics), or the encouraging of right habits and the shunning of vices (virtue ethics). It seeks to answer questions, such as "How should we live?" and "Should our goal be happiness, knowledge, or virtue?" One of the four main branches of philosophy. *See also* epistemology; logic; metaphysics.

Eucharist—*See* Lord's Supper; Lord's Supper, views.

Eutychianism—*See* Christ's unity.

Evangelical Theological Society—*See* Henry, Carl F. H.; inerrancy.

evangelicalism—a conservative movement in modern Christianity stressing conversion, biblical authority, orthodox doctrine, and evangelism. Evangelicals hold that Scripture is the chief authority for faith and life. Salvation is by faith in Christ, crucified, risen, and coming again. Evangelicalism emphasizes the worldwide preaching of the gospel. It traces its origins to the Reformation, pietism, Puritanism, and revivalism. In the United States in the mid-twentieth century, evangelicalism came out of the controversy between fundamentalism and liberalism. Evangelicals separated from fundamentalists by continuing to hold to conservative theology while engaging scholarship and society. Today evangelicalism is a worldwide movement composed of many local churches, denominations, and institutions. *See also* Eastern Orthodoxy; ecumenism; neoorthodoxy; Reformation; Roman Catholicism.

evangelism—*See* gospel; Great Commission; mission.

evil desires—*See* indwelling sin; temptation.

evolution—*See* humanity, origin.

ex nihilo—Latin phrase applied to creation, meaning "out of nothing." Refers to the beginning of God's work of creation, when he used no previously existing material (Rom 4:17; Heb 11:3). *See also* creation.

exaltation of Christ—*See* Christ's states of humiliation and exaltation.

exclusivism/inclusivism/pluralism—three views concerning whether the unevangelized need the gospel. Pluralism denies Christ's uniqueness and holds that all religions lead to God. Therefore, there is no need for world evangelism. Scripture excludes pluralism, for Jesus claims to be the only way to the Father (John 14:6), and the apostles teach that his is the only name that saves (Acts 4:12). Both exclusivism and inclusivism maintain that Jesus's death and resurrection are the only way to God. But they differ on the necessity of the lost believing the gospel. Exclusivism says Jesus is the only Savior and people must believe in him to be saved. Inclusivism agrees that he is the only Savior but holds that people can be saved by Jesus without hearing the gospel. Some inclusivists say this occurs when people in the world's religions sincerely seek God. Others say the lost can be saved by Jesus as they respond favorably to general revelation or conscience. Inclusivism is a significant error. Scripture points to special revelation as the object of saving faith (Gen 15:6), and as the biblical story moves to the New Testament, saving faith is always directed to Jesus Christ (Acts 16:31; Rom 4:16–25; 10:9–17; Gal 2:15–16; 3:16). *See also* application of salvation; Christ's deity; conversion; faith; gospel; Great Commission; Rahner, Karl; revelation.

excommunication—*See* church, marks.

exegesis—careful study of biblical passages and the foundation of all good theology. Includes attending to both the historical and the literary context of each passage. Involves noting a passage's literary genre and strategies specific to that genre. *See also* doctrine; hermeneutics; systematic theology; theological method.

existence of God, arguments for the—rational proofs for God's existence, the "Five Ways" that Thomas Aquinas set forth in his *Summa theologiae.* Aquinas did not intend to prove the orthodox doctrine of God but proposed his Five Ways as a first stage of belief in God. (1) Everything in motion was set in motion by something else, so there must be a first "unmoved Mover." (2) Nothing causes itself, so there must be a first Cause that is not caused. (3) Everything that exists depends on something else for its existence, so there must be an independent Being. (4) There are degrees of perfection, so there must be a Being of absolute perfection. (5) The world evidences much design, so there must be an intelligent Designer. *See also* Aquinas, Thomas; creation.

existentialism—a twentieth-century philosophy that rejected an older emphasis on essence and instead emphasized individual existence. Its goal was for each person to find self, significance, and authenticity through the exercise of free will, good choices, and the acceptance of personal responsibility. Discarding the older idea of objective truth, existentialism taught that people must search to define their own values and goals. Life is irrational and sometimes bleak, and individuals must struggle to find their way without rules or traditions. Jean Paul Sartre popularized existentialism internationally. *See also* epistemology; truth; truthfulness of God.

exorcism—the casting out of evil spirits (demons) by God's power. Jesus (Matt 8:16; Mark 7:25–30) and his apostles performed exorcisms (Acts 8:7; 16:16–18) on people possessed by demons. Demons possess unsaved people when they inhabit and control them. *See also* angels; Christ's saving work, biblical images; Holy Spirit's works; Satan and demons.

experience—*See* theology, sources.

expiation—*See* atonement; Christ's saving work, biblical images; justification; propitiation.

external call—*See* calling.

extreme unction—*See* ordinances or sacraments; Roman Catholicism.

Ff

faith—trusting in Christ as Savior and Lord for salvation. Without faith we cannot please God (Heb 11:6). Faith is necessary for salvation, and we are saved through faith in Christ (John 14:6; Acts 4:12). Faith involves knowledge, assent, and trust. We must hear and *know* the facts of the gospel. But knowing the facts is not enough, for many know the truth but do not believe it. We must *assent* to the gospel as God's truth. But accepting the facts of the gospel is insufficient. We must *trust* Jesus and his finished work to be saved. Faith is only as reliable as its object. Faith can be misplaced, for we may trust in unworthy objects. However, faith in Christ crucified and risen saves: "Faith comes from what is heard, and what is heard comes through the message about Christ" (Rom 10:17). There is initial saving faith (John 20:31; Acts 16:31) and lifelong faith (2 Cor 5:7; Gal 2:20). Faith is God's gift (John 6:44; Acts 13:48), but also human beings' responsibility (Matt 8:10; Acts 16:31). *See also* application of salvation; conversion; exclusivism/inclusivism/pluralism; repentance.

faithfulness—*See* sanctification; spiritual disciplines; virtues, Christian.

faithfulness of God—God's reliability in his character, actions, and words. He is the faithful God, who keeps his covenant with his people. His faithfulness means he provides for us when we are tempted, forgives us when we repent, and assures us that he will sustain us to the end. That God is faithful means we can fully trust him and his Word in all circumstances (Ps 89:1–3; Lam 3:21–24; 1 Cor 1:8–9; 1 Thess 5:23–24). *See also* assurance of salvation; covenant(s); immutability of God; repentance; Scripture, attributes; temptation; truth.

fall, the—Adam's descent into sin, which brought God's curse, with cata-strophic results for the world of humanity, including its own sin, inability, total depravity, guilt, corruption, death, suffering, and estrangement. After the fall, human beings were born sinners (Ps 51:5). Sin is both the state in which we live and the evil acts that we commit. The fall brought inabil-ity, so that sinners cannot rescue themselves from the effects of sin (2 Cor 4:3–4). Adam's original sin brought total depravity to the human race. This does not mean that we are as bad as we could be; rather, all parts of us and our lives are contaminated by sin (Rom 1:21–22). Original sin brought guilt—legal condemnation before a holy God (Rom 5:18)—and corruption—sin's moral defilement of lives (Gal 5:19–21). As God warned Adam, sin brought death, and ever since, all human beings have died. There was no suffering in Eden, but suffering is common in our world since the fall. Adam's sin brought estrangement from God, so he and Eve hid from God (Gen 3:8). Adam's posterity are also estranged from God and one another and need grace and reconciliation, which only God can bring. *See also* death; grace of God; guilt; sin; theodicy; total depravity.

fallen angels—*See* angels; exorcism; Satan and demons.

family of God—*See* adoption; church, pictures.

fear of God—believers' respect, awe, and honor of God, distinguished from unbelievers' terror of divine judgment. *See also* holiness of God; wrath of God.

federal headship—*See* Christ's saving work, biblical images; sin; substitution.

fellowship—partnership and sharing between God and believers and between believers. The term describes the warm, inviting relationship that God initiates with Christians: "Our fellowship is with the Father and with his Son Jesus Christ" (1 John 1:3; see also 1 Cor 1:9). Paul adds that we have fellowship with the Holy Spirit too (2 Cor 13:13). Those living in sin do not experience fellowship with God unless they confess their sins (1 John 1:6, 9). If believers live for God, they enjoy fellowship with him and one another, and the basis for this companionship is the fact that "the blood of Jesus his Son cleanses us from all sin" (v. 7). The early church devoted themselves to fellowship as they served and prayed together, encouraging one another (Acts 2:42). *See also* Christ's saving work, biblical images; reconciliation; virtues, Christian.

Fernando, Aijith (1948–)—has served with Youth for Christ in his native Sri Lanka for more than thirty-five years. He has contributed to a theology of suffering and hope for the urban poor, to whom he has been active in ministry. He penned the award-winning *The Call to Joy and Pain* and *Sharing the Truth in Love*. His latest book is *Discipling a Multi-Cultural World*. *See also* mission.

fiat creationism—*See* creation; humanity, origin.

filled with the Holy Spirit—*See* Holy Spirit's filling.

First and the Last—*See* Christ's names and titles.

firstborn from the dead—*See* Christ's names and titles.

firstfruits—*See* Holy Spirit's names and descriptions.

five points of Calvinism—*See* Calvinism.

flesh, the—*See* sin; temptation.

foreknowledge—God's knowledge of the future from the beginning. Arminians and Calvinists define God's foreknowledge differently with reference to God's electing people for salvation. Arminians hold that God chooses people for salvation based on his foreseeing their *faith* in Christ. Calvinists hold that foreknowledge refers to God's foreknowing his *people* (loving them beforehand) and choosing them for salvation. Scripture mentions "foreknow"/"foreknowledge" and salvation in Rom 8:29; 11:2; and 1 Pet 1:2. *See also* compatibilism; election; free will; incompatibilism; omniscience of God; open theism; sovereignty of God.

foreordination—God's arranging of all events before they occur: "I am God, and no one is like me. I declare the end from the beginning" (Isa 46:9–10). His foreordination is all-encompassing, for he "works out everything in agreement with the purpose of his will" (Eph 1:11). *See also* election; sovereignty of God.

forgiveness of sins—*See* gospel; justification; new covenant.

foundationalism—a theory of knowledge that seeks to build knowledge on a secure basis (foundation). Foundations vary, and while Descartes based his foundationalism on reason, Friedrich Schleiermacher—the father of modern theology—based his on experience. Postmodernism is anti-foundationalist in its rejection of any solid foundation for knowledge. *See also* epistemology; modernism; postmodernism; relativism; truth; truthfulness of God.

free will—term encompassing both freedom of choice and true freedom. At creation, God gave Adam and Eve both of these. Freedom of choice is the ability to make spontaneous choices according to the inclinations of the will. This is an unlosable part of humanness. True freedom is relational; it is the ability to know, love, serve, and enjoy God as he intended. Because of Adam's original sin, humans lost true freedom (John 8:34). Although we retain freedom of choice, we are guilty before God, and sin defiles our lives (Mark 7:20–23). Further, we suffer inability. Due to Adam's sin and our own sins, we cannot rescue ourselves (Matt 19:24–26). On their own, in fact, fallen human beings cannot trust Christ as Savior. They need the Holy Spirit to work in their hearts to come to know Christ. The Spirit overcomes their spiritual deadness and makes them alive to God (John 3:8; Eph 2:4–5). In so doing, God restores to them a measure of true freedom. Like Adam and Eve in the garden, Christians know, love, and serve God. But sin remains in them, and they do not love him wholeheartedly but grow in true freedom (2 Cor 3:16–18). The final state of affairs will be best because, when resurrected on the new earth, believers will have true freedom perfected. Our situation will be better than that of our first parents, for we will be unable to sin. As always, we will have freedom of choice, but as perfected human beings we will be in a positive relationship with God and will always choose his glory and never choose to sin. We will serve God in the true freedom for which he created us (Rev 22:3–4). *See also* compatibilism; foreknowledge; incompatibilism; sin; sovereignty of God.

fruit of the Spirit—*See* Holy Spirit's ministries; sanctification; virtues, Christian.

functional view of image—*See* image of God (*imago Dei*).

fundamentalism—a conservative movement in American Protestantism that began in the late nineteenth century. It arose in reaction to biblical criticism, evolution, and liberalism, which grew in popularity in American churches and seminaries. In 1920, the term *fundamentalist* was named after *The Fundamentals*, a series of pamphlets that condemned modernist theories and reaffirmed scriptural authority. Fundamentalists affirmed "fundamentals" of the faith. These included inerrancy, the virgin birth, miracles, atonement in Jesus's blood, the resurrection of the body, and the Second Coming. *See also* Eastern Orthodoxy; ecumenism; evangelicalism; humanity, origin; neoorthodoxy; Reformation; Roman Catholicism.

Gg

Gehenna—*See* hell.

general revelation—*See* revelation.

gentleness—*See* virtues, Christian.

gifts of the Spirit—*See* Holy Spirit's gifts.

glorification—God sharing his glory with his people while maintaining the Creator/creature distinction. Created in God's image to worship and display him, we refused to acknowledge his glory, sought our own, and forfeited the glory he intended for us. But because of God's overcoming grace, he has given us glory in Christ in the past, present, and future. The image of God, in which he created us (Gen 1:26–27), still exists, though tarnished. It is gradually restored in Christ (Col 3:9–10; Eph 4:22–24). It will be perfected only when Christ, the true image (2 Cor 4:4; Col 1:15), powerfully conforms us to his image in resurrection (Phil 3:21). Meanwhile, we have Christ in us, "the hope of glory" (Col 1:27). In fact, our present sufferings do not compare "with the glory that is going to be revealed to us" (Rom 8:18). Amazingly, glorification means God will enable resurrected saints to see and partake of Christ's glory and be transformed by it (1 Pet 5:1). Though at death our spirits are "made perfect" (Heb 12:23), in glorification our *bodies* are redeemed (Rom 8:23). There will be continuity between our present bodies and our resurrection bodies (v. 11), but there will also be discontinuity, for our new bodies will be imperishable, glorious, powerful, and immortal (1 Cor 15:42–54). They will be both physical and "spiritual" (v. 44), ruled by the Spirit. As believers, we are a microcosm of the final redemption of the cosmos, the macrocosm: "the creation itself will also be set free from the bondage to decay into the glorious freedom of God's children" (Rom 8:21). God will fulfill his purposes for creation by delivering it from the curse (Rev 22:3) and perfecting us (1 Thess 5:23) and it (2 Pet 3:13). *See also* application of salvation; heaven; new heavens and new earth.

glory—*See* glorification; glory of God; heaven.

glory of God—God's majesty, worth, beauty, and splendor. At times the term refers to an attribute, or a summary attribute, of God (Ps 24:8–10; Acts 7:2). Glory often expresses God's special presence, as in the glory cloud (Exod 13:21–22; 24:16–18) or the tabernacle (Exod 29:43; 40:34–38). Even more, the glory of God frames the biblical story and worldview. Scripture speaks of God's glory in at least six ways. First, only he has inherent glory (Isa 42:8). Second, God reveals his glory in creation (Ps 19:1), providence (Ps 104:31), human image bearers (Ps 8:4–5), and redemption (Exod 14:13–18; Acts 3:13–15). Third, believers glorify him (Ps 115:1; Rev 19:1). Fourth, God receives their glory (Ps 29:1–2; Rev 4:9–11). Fifth, he shares his glory with believers in salvation (2 Cor 3:18; 2 Thess 2:14). Sixth, all this redounds to God's glory (Rom 11:36). *See also* attributes of God; communicable attributes of God; glorification.

glossolalia—*See* speaking in tongues.

Gnosticism—influential second-century Greek heretical movements that the church condemned. Gnostics held to a higher, secret knowledge (Gk., *gnosis*) apart from Scripture and felt that spiritual realities are good and physical ones evil. Therefore, Gnosticism denied the Son of God's incarnation and humanity. Jesus only appeared to have a body (Docetism). Gnostic ethics went in opposite directions: denial of physical appetites (asceticism) and indulgence in them (hedonism). *See also* asceticism; Christ's humanity; Christ's humanity, denials; Christ's incarnation.

God, names of—terms used by God in Scripture to reveal his identity, including these important Old Testament names: *Adonai* is related to a word that means "lord" when it refers to human masters. But *adonai* almost always refers to the "Lord," our heavenly Master (Isa 6:1). "Lord of Armies" ("of Hosts") portrays God as Ruler of the heavenly armies (Isa 47:4), who fights for his people (1 Sam 17:45). *Elohim* is a common name sometimes applied to pagan gods and sometimes to the true God as the strong One (Gen 1:1). *Yahweh* ("Lord" or "God") is the most frequent name for God. It is his proper name and speaks of his covenant relationship to his people (Exod 3:13–15). *See also* Christ's names and titles; Holy Spirit's names and descriptions.

"God-breathed"—*See* inspiration.

godliness—*See* virtues, Christian.

golden rule, the—a common title for Jesus's saying, "Whatever you want others to do for you, do also the same for them" (Matt 7:12; see also Luke 6:31). This adage, not unique to Christianity, contains much wisdom. We certainly want others to treat us well, and Jesus makes this the gauge of our treatment of them, teaching us to be kind. The way Jesus finishes the saying is unique to Christianity: "for this is the Law and the Prophets." Jesus pronounces this saying to be the heart of Old Testament ethics—the law of love.

Good Shepherd—*See* Christ's names and titles.

good works—deeds done in obedience to God that show love for him and neighbor. Good works are not the basis for salvation. Instead, God saves humans based on grace through faith in Christ (Eph 2:8–9; Gal 2:16). Thinking that salvation is by works is an insult to Jesus's death and resurrection (Gal 2:21). God saved us to do good works that he planned (Eph 2:10; Titus 3:4–8). Good works do not merit God's favor (Isa 64:6) but are the result of it. Having become God's children, we show our love for Jesus by keeping his commandments (John 14:15). Such good works are the result of the Father's work in us (Phil 2:15) and the fruit of the Holy Spirit (Gal 5:22–26). *See also* Christ's saving work; Holy Spirit's ministries; sanctification; virtues, Christian.

goodness—*See* virtues, Christian.

goodness of God—God's care for and kindness toward all his creation, including humans, animals, and wildflowers, as well as his good gifts to both believing and unbelieving humans. God's goodness led Israel to the Promised Land, where he showed special care for the poor. Unlike that of humans, God's goodness lasts forever. He reveals his generosity in creation, but it shines in redemption. We praise God for his goodness and reflect it by loving and praying for enemies (Gen 1:31; Matt 5:45; Acts 14:17; Jas 1:17). *See also* common grace; poor, the; problem of evil; providence.

good news—*See* gospel.

gospel—(1) the message of the good news of salvation in Christ; (2) *capitalized*: a genre of New Testament literature that tells of Christ's life, death, and resurrection: the Gospels of Matthew, Mark, Luke, and John. The gospel as message centers on what Jesus did for us and our response to him. Paul summarizes the gospel as Christ's death for sinners, his resurrection, and the necessity of people's believing in him for salvation. The gospel thus includes the work of Christ, the need for faith, and God's promises of forgiveness and eternal life (John 3:16; Rom 10:9–10; 1 Cor 15:1–4). *See also* Great Commission; preaching; Scripture.

gospel call—*See* calling.

governmental view of the atonement—*See* Christ's saving work, historical views.

grace of God—God's deep compassion for all, especially his people, leading to his giving them undeserved favor and thus heaven instead of hell. Grace typifies each person of the Trinity. God is gracious to unbelievers and offers them the gospel. His grace brings salvation in all its glory. God's grace drives the Christian life, for grace is his unmerited love *and* his power, called enabling grace. God's grace pertains to the past, present, and future: we are saved by God's grace, live by his grace, and long for his grace. His goal is to display his grace forever in his church. We must, then, set our hope on the grace that Christ will bring at his return (Exod 34:6; Ps 84:10–11; Eph 2:4–10; Jas 4:6; 1 Pet 1:13). *See also* common grace; love of God.

Great Commission—Jesus's command to make disciples worldwide (Matt 28:18–20). He prefaces this command with his universal authority as Lord (v. 18). Universality and particularity mark the Great Commission. Universality: Jesus has all authority, commands discipleship of all nations, and instructs the keeping of all his commands, promising to be with his disciples "always, to the end of the age" (v. 20). Particularity: Jesus alone is Lord and alone is worthy of worship, his teachings are binding, and he is ever-present with his people as they fulfill his mission. The Commission's essence is its command to disciple all nations. Disciples live in community, in fellowship with Jesus the Teacher and one another as followers. Making disciples of all nations expands the mission beyond Israel to all Gentiles. Three participles clarify the central command to make disciples: going, baptizing, and teaching. "Go" is the action necessary to accomplish the command of making disciples. Jesus's followers must also baptize disciples in the name of the Father, the Son, and the Holy Spirit (v. 19). Through baptism, new disciples publicly identify with Christ as Lord, with one another in Jesus's kingdom community, and with the Trinity. Making disciples also includes "teaching them to observe everything" Jesus commanded (v. 19). The disciples do not put forward their own teachings but faithfully pass on those of the Teacher. Both disciplers and new disciples must believe and practice Jesus's teachings. His people are to be focused on the multiplication of other faithful followers of Jesus among the nations. In the first snapshot of the church, this is what we see. Peter preaches the gospel, and 3,000 people believe and are baptized. Next, "[the believers] devoted themselves to the apostles' teaching, to the fellowship, to the breaking of bread, and to prayer" (Acts 2:42). From the start, the church is devoted to what Jesus taught: making disciples through going, baptizing, and teaching. *See also* baptism; Carmichael, Amy; discipleship; Eareckson Tada, Joni; mission; preaching.

great tribulation, the—*See* tribulation.

Great White Throne—*See* Last Judgment.

greatness of God—God's attribute of being of utmost importance and beyond comparison. He alone is the High and Exalted One, and there is no one like him (Exod 15:11). The Lord is unique, especially compared to the so-called gods of the nations, which are really idols (Ps 86:8–10). The Psalms praise God for the greatness of his name and person (Ps(s) 8:1, 9; 148:13) and for the greatness of his works (Ps 145:3–6). God's greatness leads us to fear him (Jer 10:6–7) and to worship him only (Ps 96:3–5; Luke 1:46–48). It moves us to submit to his sovereignty (Ps 135:5–6) and to trust in his covenant faithfulness (Neh 1:5). God's greatness also inspires us to bear witness of him to others (Ps 145:3–6). *See also* attributes of God; communicable attributes; idolatry; incommunicable attributes.

guilt—humans' deserved condemnation before God because of Adam's original sin and their own sins. Since the fall, all humans are guilty because they reject God's general revelation in creation (Rom 1:18–32), reject his general revelation in the internal law of conscience (2:14–16), and fail to live according to his special revelation in the Torah (law of God, 2:17–29). Moreover, they are guilty in Adam because of his original sin in Eden (5:16–19). Humans are universally guilty (3:19–20) by nature (by birth, Gal 2:15) and stand condemned under God's wrath. Moreover, according to John's Gospel, everyone who does not believe in Jesus is already spiritually dead (John 3:3–5), presently condemned (v. 18), and God's wrath is already on them (v. 36). Further, they do not believe because they love the darkness (vv. 19–20), and God judges them for this. *See also* fall, the; sin; theodicy; unpardonable sin.

Gutiérrez, Gustavo (1928–)—Peruvian philosopher, Dominican priest, and a founder of liberation theology. After studying in Europe, Gutiérrez returned to Peru, where the widespread poverty greatly moved him. He sought to apply "love thy neighbor" to the sin of unjust social structures. Gutiérrez wrote *A Theology of Liberation* in 1973, the foundational text of liberation theology. "Preferential option for the poor" means following Jesus in ministry among the downtrodden. Speaking and writing are not enough. "Liberating praxis" means the coming of God's kingdom in economic and spiritual freedom for the socially oppressed. Gutiérrez's ideas influenced Latin American theology, including evangelicalism's "integral mission." *See also* liberation theology; Padilla, René.

Hh

hamartiology—in Christian theology, the study of the doctrines of the fall and sin.

head of the church—*See* Christ's names and titles; church, pictures.

healing—*See* charismatic gifts; Holy Spirit's gifts.

heaven—the final state of resurrected believers on the new earth. The Bible paints six major pictures of heaven. First, heaven will be the renewal of creation. God will deliver his good creation from sin so that "there will no longer be any curse" (Rev 22:3). Then the longings of the personified creation presented in Rom 8:18–23 will be fulfilled. As resurrected believers, we will live forever under the new heavens on the new earth. We will enjoy the best of this world's culture forever in the city of God, the new Jerusalem (Rev 21:26). Although some hold that the present earth will be destroyed and that God will create a totally new earth, it is preferable to understand instead that the present earth will be renewed (Isa 65:17; 66:22; Rom 8:18–28; 2 Pet 3:10–13; Rev 21:1–5). Second, heaven will be the final stage of the kingdom of God. Though the battle rages until Christ's second coming (1 Pet 5:8), as God's people we conquer through Christ, who loved us and gave himself for us (Gal 2:20; Rev 5:5–6). When the final installment of the kingdom arrives, the struggles of the present will be past. By God's grace, believers will exercise dominion with Christ, human life will flourish (Heb 2:5–10; Rev 21:24–26), and we will serve our great King as his subjects forever (Rev 7:15). Third, heaven will be our everlasting rest. Jesus brings real rest now (Matt 11:28), but when he returns there will be no more sin or strife in the lives of individuals, families, or nations.

We will find fulfillment, eagerly serving Jesus in the perpetual Sabbath rest of the new creation (Heb 4:9–11; Rev 14:13). Fourth, in heaven we will be in God's gracious presence forever. In the Old Testament, God dwelled with his people in tabernacle and temple. Since the resurrection of Christ, the Holy Spirit dwells in believers individually and the church corporately (1 Cor 3:16; 6:19). But in that day we will experience God's presence as never before. Because of the perfect work of Christ, when he returns we will delight in God's presence, for "God himself will be with [us] and will be [our] God" (Rev 21:3). Fifth, heaven will be the final vision of God. He warns Moses that no one can see him and live (Exod 33:20). Though God gives glimpses of himself in the Old Testament (24:10–11; 34:5–8), in the end God can say of his people, "They will see his face" (Rev 22:4). Jesus pronounced the pure in heart truly happy, for "they will see God" (Matt 5:8). In the meantime, we live by faith in Jesus, not by sight (2 Cor 5:7; 1 Pet 1:8). Therefore, "we hope for what we do not see," and "we eagerly wait for it with patience" (Rom 8:25). Moreover, "when [Jesus] appears, we will be like him because we will see him as he is" (1 John 3:2). Sixth, heaven will involve our shining in glory forever (see Dan 12:3). When Christ came, the apostles saw his great "glory as the one and only Son from the Father" (John 1:14). Because of Christ's excellent person and work, Scripture describes both our present and our final salvation in terms of glory. Astonishingly, Paul describes Christians' lives as looking at Christ's glory and "being transformed into the same image from glory to glory" (2 Cor 3:18). Paul considers our present troubles in light of our future glory as "momentary light affliction" compared to "an absolutely incomparable eternal weight of glory" (4:17). Our salvation is bound up with Christ so that "when Christ, who is [our] life, appears, then [we] also will appear with him in glory" (Col 3:4). Our bodies will be raised in glory, and we will be glorified. We will behold God's glory and be transformed by it so that we partake of it (1 Cor 15:43; 1 Pet 5:1; Rev 21:10–11, 19–26). *See also* glorification; hell; new heavens and new earth; preterism; Sabbath.

heirs of God—*See* adoption.

hell—the eternal suffering of unbelievers at the hands of God, the righteous Judge. First, hell is a place where people suffer the just penalty for their sin. Punishment is the Bible's primary picture of hell (2 Thess 1:5–9; Rev 20:10–15). In the end, God's justice will prevail to punish the wicked and comfort persecuted believers. Second, hell as destruction or death also plays a central role. Jesus (Matt 7:13–14), John (John 3:16; Rev 21:8), and Paul (Rom 6:23; 2 Thess 1:9) teach it. Destruction and death signify the final and utter loss, ruin, or waste of the unsaved. A third picture of hell, banishment, is taught by Jesus (Matt 7:21–23; 8:12; 13:41–42) and John (Rev 22:14–15). Banishment conveys dreadful exclusion from God's grace due to his active judgment and stresses the desolation and finality of the predicament. Fourth, Scripture frequently says that those in hell experience suffering (Matt 3:12; 5:29–30) like that of a fiery furnace, bearing unimaginable sorrow and pain. Jesus frequently speaks of hell as suffering, using his favorite word for it, *Gehenna* (from the Hebrew for "valley of Hinnom," where children were sacrificed to Molech in the Old Testament, Matt 5:22, 29–30; 18:9; Luke 12:5). The pain induces "weeping and gnashing of teeth" (Matt 22:13; 24:51; 25:30). Hebrews warns that hell is fearful and dreadful (Heb 10:27–31). John's portrait is unforgettable. Those in hell will feel the full force of God's fury (Rev 14:10). They will be "tormented with fire" (14:10–11), endlessly suffering constantly (v. 11; 20:10). This suffering is conscious, for these biblical images imply that those in hell will know that they are suffering just punishment. The biblical teaching is straightforward: hell is eternal. The historic church has confessed that the suffering of the lost in hell will have no end. This is contrary to universalism and annihilationism. Universalism is the view that in the end everyone will be saved. Annihilationism, also known as conditional immortality, or conditionalism for short, holds that the wicked will temporarily suffer for their sins in hell. When they have paid their debt, God will exterminate them, and they will exist no more. Universalism and annihilationism are to be opposed because of Scripture's clear teaching that hell's punishment is never-ending. Daniel contrasts "eternal life" with "disgrace and eternal contempt" as fates of the resurrected righteous and unrighteous, respectively (Dan 12:2). Jesus appeals to Isa 66:22, 24 when warning his hearers that hell involves "unquenchable fire" in a place "where their worm does not die and the fire is not quenched" (Mark 9:43, 48). In the most famous passage on hell, Jesus equates the final fate of unsaved human beings with that of "the devil and his angels"—"eternal fire" (Matt 25:41). Revelation 20:10 is explicit: "They will be tormented day and night forever and ever." Jesus contrasts the destinies of the lost and the saved: "eternal punishment" and "eternal life" (Matt 25:46). He depicts both destinies in a single sentence as "eternal." Clearly, the punishment of the lost is without end. John powerfully testifies to the eternity of hell. Idolaters "will be tormented with fire and sulfur . . . , and the smoke of their torment will go up forever and ever" (Rev 14:10–11). Rather than being annihilated, the lost have "no rest, day or night" (v. 11). The endlessness of this punishment is confirmed by the assertion said of Satan, among others: "The devil . . . was thrown into the lake of fire and sulfur . . . and they will be tormented day and night forever and ever" (Rev 20:10). Five verses later, John teaches (agreeing with Matt 25:41) that unsaved human beings will share the devil's fate and be "thrown into the lake of fire" (Rev 20:15). Regardless of what we might desire to be true, Scripture's witness is plain: the suffering of unbelievers in body and soul in hell will never end. In rejecting God, they will never experience his glorious presence or the ultimate covenant blessing—eternal life. *See also* annihilationism; guilt; heaven; preterism; sin; universalism.

Henry, Carl F. H. (1913–2003)—American evangelical Baptist theologian who helped lead evangelicalism in the mid- to late-twentieth century. He helped create the Evangelical Theological Society to encourage academic dialogue among evangelicals and was founding editor of *Christianity Today* as a scholarly voice for evangelical Christianity and a challenge to the liberal *Christian Century*. In 1978 he signed the Chicago Statement on Biblical Inerrancy. Henry finished his most famous work, the six-volume *God, Revelation, and Authority*, in 1983. *See also* Chicago Statement on Biblical Inerrancy; inerrancy; inspiration; truth.

heresy—false teaching that contradicts orthodoxy. There are degrees of error, and some errors are more serious than others. Errors concerning the person of Christ or the way of salvation are more serious than those concerning church government or timing on last things—matters on which Christians can disagree without compromising biblical teaching to do so. Heresy is serious error concerning vital truths, such as who God is, the deity of Christ, or the gospel. Someone holding to heresy is a *heretic*. Paul and Peter condemn heresy (Gal 1:6–9; 2 Pet 2:1). An elder must hold to "the faithful message" of the gospel so as to be able to promote "sound teaching" and "to refute those who contradict it" (Titus 1:9). *See also* doctrine; systematic theology; truth.

hermeneutics—the art and science of biblical interpretation. Biblical interpretation encompasses both general and special hermeneutics. General hermeneutics pertains to the interpretation of any literature. It deals with grammar and syntax, historical background, context, speech figures, and genre. Special hermeneutics pertains to the interpretation of Scripture. To matters of general hermeneutics, it adds redemptive history, prophecy and fulfillments, type and antitype, and relation to Christ. Recent studies in hermeneutics have drawn attention to the relationships between author, text, and original and later readers. Hermeneutics differs from exegesis, which is applying hermeneutics to the actual interpretation of biblical texts. *See also* exegesis; systematic theology.

historic premillennialism—*See* millennium.

historical theology—the study of the church's understanding of Scripture and its teaching over the centuries. Believers today stand in the historical stream of God's people throughout church history and can learn much from its leading thinkers. We should depart from the church's historic positions only with caution, when persuaded by the Bible or evident reason. We read Scripture not only as individuals but in community and taught by the past. While historical church teachings and creeds are not as authoritative as Scripture, they are an important resource for theology. *See also* doctrine; systematic theology; theological method.

holiness—believers' actual ethical purity. God alone is absolutely holy— separate from everything else and entirely sinless. Only he consecrates things and people. He sets apart his people from the realm of sin, constituting them saints, and he will one day perfect them in holiness. In the meantime, he gives them the Holy Spirit and enables them to make progress in actual godliness. He works in believers to purify them from evil and impurity. He liberates them from bondage to sin and frees them to serve him (Matt 5:48; 1 Pet 1:14–16). *See also* sanctification; spiritual disciplines; spirituality; virtues, Christian.

holiness movement—a mid-nineteenth-century American movement in John Wesley's tradition that held to a post-conversion experience of entire sanctification and Christian perfection in love. *See also* Methodists; Wesley, John; Wesleyanism.

holiness of God—God's status as both unique and sinless. He is distinct from all else, and there is no one like him. God is also entirely pure and sinless, separate from anything unholy. God's moral holiness exposes our sinfulness and condemns us. But holy God is also full of mercy, and he forgives all who trust his Son as Savior. Further, God commands his redeemed people to live holy lives. We will praise God's holiness for all eternity (Exod 15:11; Ps 99:2–5; Isa 6:3; 1 Pet 1:14–16). *See also* fear of God; hell; holiness; mercy of God; righteousness (justice) of God; sanctification.

holiness of the church—*See* church, attributes; church, marks.

holy orders—*See* ordinances or sacraments; Roman Catholicism.

Holy Spirit—*See* Holy Spirit's personality.

Holy Spirit and evangelism—*See* Holy Spirit's works.

Holy Spirit and Jesus's life and ministry—*See* Holy Spirit's works.

Holy Spirit and the Word—*See* Holy Spirit's works.

Holy Spirit's deity—the Holy Spirit's identity as a divine person alongside the Father and the Son, depicted in at least four ways in Scripture. First, the Holy Spirit has divine qualities, as his names reveal. He is "the Spirit of truth" because he reveals Jesus (John 14:17; 16:13–15). He is the "Holy Spirit," for his name connects him to God's holiness in a way fitting for God. God's Spirit exercises divine power when he does miracles through Paul, as in Rom 15:19. The Spirit also possesses the attributes of eternity (Heb 9:14) and divine knowledge (1 Cor 2:10–11). Second, the Spirit does divine works, taking part in creation (Gen 1:1–2), the writing of Scripture (2 Pet 1:20–21), and salvation. He plays a part in raising

Jesus from the dead (Rom 1:4). The Spirit unites us to Christ (1 Cor 12:13) and applies to us adoption (Rom 8:15), regeneration (John 3:8), sanctification (2 Thess 2:13), and justification (1 Cor 6:11). He will also play a role in our resurrection (Rom 8:11). Only God indwells his people, and Jesus predicts that the Spirit will indwell us (John 14:16–17), and Paul says that the Spirit indeed does so (Rom 8:9; 2 Tim 1:14). Third, the Spirit's name is interchanged with God's. This is implied when Peter says that when Ananias lied "to the Holy Spirit," he lied not "to people but to God" (Acts 5:3–4). Paul asserts that Christians are "God's temple" (1 Cor 3:16) and a "temple of the Holy Spirit" (6:19). This interchangeability shows that the Spirit's name is equated with God's. Fourth, the Spirit is linked with the Father and the Son as only God can be. In the Great Commission, Jesus tells the disciples to baptize "in the name of the Father and of the Son and of the Holy Spirit" (Matt 28:19). The Spirit is here combined with the other two persons of the Trinity in a way proper for God alone. In Paul's benediction, the Son, the Father, and the Spirit give divine blessings, showing the Spirit's deity (2 Cor 13:13). *See also* Trinity.

Holy Spirit's filling—the Holy Spirit's enabling believers to grow in maturity as they yield to his control over their lives. Although filling can refer to initial reception of the Spirit (Acts 9:17), it most often speaks of believers' ongoing relationship with him; thus, there are multiple fillings in Acts (2:4; 4:8, 31; 9:17; 13:9, 52). It often refers to divine enablement to speak and witness for God (Luke 1:41–42, 67; Acts 4:8, 31; 13:9–11). Those who walk with the Lord while filled with the Spirit are sometimes characterized as "full" of the Holy Spirit (Acts 6:3, 5; 7:55; 11:24). Paul commands Christians, "Don't get drunk with wine, which leads to reckless living, but be filled by the Spirit" (Eph 5:18). *See also* Holy Spirit's indwelling; Holy Spirit's ministries.

Holy Spirit's gifts—the Spirit's spiritual endowments and abilities given to God's people. First Corinthians 12–14 teaches us seven truths about spiritual gifts. First, we see the familiar divine sovereignty/human responsibility paradox. The Spirit sovereignly assigns gifts "as he wills" (12:11), and Paul commands us to "desire spiritual gifts" (14:1). When we covet gifts we do not have, we must submit to the Spirit's sovereignty. And when we are inactive, we must obey God's call to serve him by using our gifts. Second, the Corinthians needed basic spiritual discernment, so Paul warns, "No one speaking by the Spirit of God says, 'Jesus is cursed,' and no one can say, 'Jesus is Lord,' except by the Holy Spirit" (12:3). Third, our spiritual gifts correspond to the unity and diversity of the Trinity: "Now there are different gifts, but the same Spirit. There are different ministries, but the same Lord. And there are different activities, but the same God produces each gift in each person" (vv. 4–6). There is one Holy Spirit, one Lord Jesus, and one God the Father. And church unity is built on the unity of the Trinity. The different gifts, ministries, and activities reflect differences between the three persons. And there is a process: the same Spirit's different gifts are used in different ministries to serve the same Lord Jesus, as the same Father empowers the gifts. When we serve the church, the Trinity uses us to bless others. Fourth, Paul gives the purpose of spiritual gifts: the Spirit gives them "for the common good" (v. 7). Peter agrees: God has given each of us at least one spiritual gift. We must "use it to serve others, as good stewards of the varied grace of God" (1 Pet 4:10). Gifts are expressions of God's grace, given us that we might serve others and benefit them (Rom 12:6–8). Fifth, Paul compares the unity in diversity of our physical bodies to the unity in diversity that the Spirit brings to the church (Rom 12:4–5; 1 Cor 12:12–13). Ordinary church members are neither unnecessary nor unimportant (1 Cor 12:14–20). And members in the limelight are not more necessary or important than others (vv. 21–24). God wills "that there would be no division in the body, but that the members would have the same concern for each other" (v. 25). Sixth, mutual love is imperative for the gifts to work properly in the body of Christ. Spectacular gifts without love are "nothing" (1 Cor 13:1–3). Paul's description of love is both delightful and too high for us to attain without the Spirit's working (vv. 4–7). Unlike spiritual gifts, love endures forever (vv. 8–12). We must not underrate love, for it is greater than faith and hope (v. 13). Seventh, prophecy and tongues call for care. Paul urges first-century believers to pursue love and spiritual gifts, especially prophecy (1 Cor 14:1, 39), to edify the church (v. 12). Prophecy was more profitable in the first-century church than tongues-speaking (vv. 2–25). Prophecy is spoken to people with the mind, not the spirit, to edify, encourage, and teach them (vv. 3–4, 31). Prophecy is a sign for unbelievers that God uses to demonstrate his reality to them (vv. 22–25). Tongues are spoken to God (v. 28) with the spirit, not the mind (v. 14), in mysteries by the Spirit (v. 2) to edify the speaker (vv. 4, 28). When tongues are interpreted, they edify the church (v. 5), but uninterpreted tongues do not (vv. 5–12). Paul speaks in tongues, but not in church without interpretation (vv. 15–19). Paul says that the church is not to forbid speaking in tongues (v. 39). He insists on order in worship services, and all must be done for edification (vv. 26–39). He gives rules for speaking in tongues: speakers are limited to three per meeting; they must speak one at a time; and interpretation is necessary (vv. 27–28). No more than three prophets may speak, and the others must weigh what they say (vv. 29–33). They too must speak one at a time (v. 31), and it is God's will that speakers be under control (vv. 32–33, 40). Evangelicals largely agree on primary matters concerning the gifts but disagree on secondary ones. We agree that certain gifts have ceased, specifically apostles and prophets as ones who speak authoritative revelation from God. We also agree that certain gifts continue, including service, teaching, exhorting, giving, leading, and showing mercy (Rom 12:6–8). We disagree concerning the cessation or continuation of the so-called sign gifts, including healing, miracles, prophecy, and tongues (1 Cor 12:9–10). We should agree that no one spiritual gift is essential for either salvation or service, for all the Corinthians were baptized with the Spirit, though not all of them spoke in tongues (1 Cor 12:13, 30). *See also* baptism of the Holy Spirit; charismatic gifts; Holy Spirit's filling; Holy Spirit's ministries; Holy Spirit's works; Pentecostalism; speaking in tongues.

Holy Spirit's indwelling—the Holy Spirit's taking up residence in and with believers in a special relationship. Paul teaches that the Trinity makes his home in and with God's people as individuals and as the church. Paul usually ascribes indwelling to the Spirit (e.g., John 14:16–17; Rom 8:9–11; 1 Cor 3:16), but does so six times to the Son (Rom 8:10; 2 Cor 13:5; Gal 2:20; Eph 3:17; Col 1:27, 3:11) and twice to the Father (2 Cor 6:16; Eph 2:22). God loves his people and draws very close to them, even indwelling them. Indwelling is ongoing union with Christ. *See also* Holy Spirit's filling; Holy Spirit's ministries.

Holy Spirit's ministries—the Holy Spirit's activities toward believers, especially his uniting us to Christ and empowering us to live for him. As the bond of our union with Christ, the Spirit baptizes us into Christ's body (1 Cor 12:13). The Spirit is indispensable for salvation, for he indwells every Christian; those who lack the Spirit do not belong to Christ (Rom 8:9). Further, the Spirit brings about the aspects of salvation occurring in union with Christ: regeneration (John 3:8; Eph 2:4–5), justification (1 Cor 6:11; 2 Cor 5:21), adoption (Gal 3:26–27; Rom 8:15), sanctification (Rom 6:3–5; 2 Thess 2:13), preservation (Rom 8:38–39; Eph 4:30), and glorification (Rom 8:17; 1 Pet 4:13). Also, through many gracious ministries, the Spirit enables us as the church to live for God: indwelling, empowering, producing fruit, providing leaders, enabling worship, and giving spiritual gifts. The Spirit indwells us as individuals (1 Cor 6:19–20) and as the church (3:16–17), assuring us of God's love (Gal 4:6). The same Spirit who empowered Jesus in his earthly ministry (Acts 10:38), atonement (Heb 9:14), and resurrection (Rom 1:4) strengthens us to live for him. The Spirit energizes the church by giving spiritual gifts (1 Cor 12:11) and empowering us in difficult circumstances (Phil 1:19), for witness (Acts 1:8), and for evangelism (Rom 15:18–19). The Spirit produces fruit in us (Gal 5:22–24) as we walk by the Spirit (5:16, 25) and trust and obey him. He enables us to love (5:13–14; 6:2) and to avoid interpersonal sins (5:15, 26). The fruit of the Spirit clashes with the works of the flesh, which include sexual (v. 19), religious (v. 20), interpersonal (vv. 20–21), and overindulgent (v. 21) sins. Among the fruit, love is first and foremost; peace is harmony among church members; and the rest also contribute to love and harmony: "joy, patience, kindness, goodness, faithfulness, gentleness, and self-control" (vv. 22–23). The Spirit guides leaders for Christ's church. He appoints (Acts 20:28) and enables (2 Cor 3:6) us and our leaders to engage effectively in new covenant ministry. He gives us wisdom, faith, power, and joy for ministry (Acts 6:3, 5, 8; 13:52), enables us to speak for God (Acts 1:8), gives us wisdom for decision-making (Acts 15:28–29), enables us to guard the gospel (2 Tim 1:13–14), enables our worship (Eph 5:18–20), and helps us to pray (Rom 8:26; Jude vv. 20–21). *See also* Holy Spirit's filling; Holy Spirit's indwelling; Holy Spirit's works; union with Christ.

Holy Spirit's names and descriptions—titles given in Scripture to the Holy Spirit that teach us his identity and roles. Some names identify him as God. He is "the Holy Spirit of God" (Eph 4:30 ESV), the "Holy Spirit" (Ps 51:11), "the Spirit of the Lord GOD" (Isa 61:1), "the Spirit of the LORD" (11:2), "the Spirit of God" (Gen 1:2), and "the seven Spirits of God" (Rev 4:5). Some names relate him to the other two persons of the Trinity. He is "the Spirit of [the] Father" (Matt 10:20), "the Spirit of [the] Son" (Gal 4:6), and "the Spirit of Christ" (Rom 8:9). Other names reveal his divine attributes. He is "the eternal Spirit" (Heb 9:14), "the Spirit of grace" (10:29), "the Spirit of holiness" (Rom 1:4), "the Spirit of life" (8:2), "the Spirit of wisdom" (Eph 1:17), "the Spirit of counsel and strength" (Isa 11:2), "the Spirit of truth" (John 14:17), and "the Spirit of glory" (1 Pet 4:14). Still other names reveal his ministries. He is "the Counselor" (John 15:26; a.k.a. "Helper," ESV; "Comforter," KJV; or "Advocate," NIV), "the Spirit of adoption" (Rom 8:15), "the firstfruits" (v. 23), "the down payment of our inheritance" (Eph 1:14), "the Spirit of . . . revelation" (v. 17), and God's "seal" (2 Cor 1:22). *See also* adoption; Paraclete; Trinity.

Holy Spirit's personality—the Holy Spirit's identity as a person, revealed in Scripture in at least three ways. First, the Spirit has personal traits, including the features of personality: intelligence, emotion, and volition. He has intelligence, for Jesus says the Spirit will teach the disciples (John 14:26). Paul says the Spirit knows God's thoughts (1 Cor 2:11). The Spirit has emotion, for he can be grieved (Eph 4:30). He has volition and bestows spiritual gifts "as he wills" (1 Cor 12:11). Second, the Spirit performs ministries that only persons perform. The Spirit takes Jesus's place (John 14:16). He perpetuates Jesus's teaching, witnesses to him, glorifies him (15:26; 16:14), and convicts people of sin (v. 8). Paul mentions the Spirit's personal ministries, such as praying (Rom 8:26), assuring (v. 16), and giving life (2 Cor 3:6). Third, the Spirit is affected as a person. He can be blasphemed (Mark 3:29), lied to (Acts 5:3), tested (v. 9), resisted (7:51), grieved (Eph 4:30), and insulted (Heb 10:29). The Holy Spirit, then, is not an impersonal force but a divine person whom believers know (John 14:17) and with whom they fellowship (2 Cor 13:14). *See also* personality of God.

Holy Spirit's works—actions the Spirit takes outside of salvation, including creating, giving Scripture, and working supernaturally in people's lives. First, the Spirit works in creation (Gen 1:1–2). Hovering over the waters (v. 2), the Spirit of God prepares the earth for human beings to inhabit, creates us, and gives us life (Job 33:4). Second, the Spirit inspires the Bible. Jesus foretold the writing of the New Testament by "the Spirit of truth" through the apostles (John 15:26; 16:13–14). Peter teaches that the Spirit is the ultimate Author of Scripture, for he worked in the prophets so that they spoke from God (2 Pet 1:21). Third, the Spirit works in people's lives in the Old Testament, the apostles, the world, and Jesus. In the Old Testament, the Holy Spirit equips and empowers master craftsman Bezalel to adorn the tabernacle (Exod 31:1–5), equips leaders (Num 27:18), empowers judges (Judg 6:34), and anoints kings (1 Sam 11:6). The Spirit enables people to prophesy, including kings (2 Sam 23:2) and prophets (Jer 19:14). The Spirit promotes spiritual renewal (2 Chr 15:1), victory over enemies (20:14), rebuke of idolatry (24:20), and rebuilding of the temple (Hag 2:5). All these are accomplished "'not by strength or by might, but by my Spirit,' says the LORD of Armies" (Zech 4:6). The Spirit makes future promises through Isaiah (61:1), Ezekiel (36:26–27), and Joel (2:28–32). He is active in the apostles' ministries. He indwells and fills them and will be their Helper forever (John 14:16–17 ESV; Acts 4:31). He gives them utterance (Matt 10:20; Luke 12:12) and wisdom (21:15) and empowers their witness about Jesus (24:49). The Spirit directs the apostles in God's work (Acts 13:2, 4), decision-making (15:28), opening doors of ministry (16:6–10), and adding believers to God's people (Eph 2:19–22). The Spirit also works in the world. Jesus promises to send the Helper to testify about him and convict the world of its need for salvation (John 15:26; 16:8–9). The Spirit invites people to come to Christ. The biblical story ends with the Spirit calling readers to Jesus for spiritual satisfaction (Rev 22:17). Moreover, the Spirit empowers people to confess Jesus as Lord (1 Cor 12:3). The Spirit also works in Jesus and his conception, baptism, temptation, teaching, healing, exorcisms, death, and resurrection. The Holy Spirit brings about his conception in Mary's womb (Luke 1:35). The Spirit has a part in Jesus's baptism and temptation. At his baptism, Jesus sees the Spirit descend on him "like a dove" (Matt 3:16). The Spirit also leads him "to be tempted by the devil" (4:1). The incarnate Son is God and man. When it is the Father's will, Christ uses divine powers. But the Father also gives Jesus the Spirit to equip him for preaching (Luke 4:18), casting out demons (Matt 12:22), and offering himself as a sacrifice for sin (Heb 9:14). The Spirit also raises Jesus from the dead (Rom 1:3–4). *See also* Holy Spirit's indwelling; Holy Spirit's ministries.

homiletics—the science and art of the planning and preaching of sermons. *See also* preaching.

homoousios—Greek term for "of the same essence or substance." Arianism held that Christ was not eternal but was God's first creature and of a different nature than the Father. The Council of Nicaea defended the deity of Christ against Arianism by affirming that Christ was *homoousios* with God the Father. *See also* Athanasius; Christ's deity; Christ's deity, denials; Council of Nicaea; Nicene Creed.

hope—a confident expectation for the future and for salvation based on God's promises and Christ's death and resurrection. Hope is faith directed toward future unseen things (Rom 8:24–25); it is based confidently on God's sovereignty and faithfulness. Christian hope patiently focuses on Christ's second coming, the resurrection, and the new heavens and new earth. *See also* faith; faithfulness of God; Second Coming; sovereignty of God.

humanity, makeup—mankind's status as created by God as holistic beings (with body and soul united), which is how we live now and is how we will live forever on the new earth. There are four main views concerning the makeup of human beings: monism, dichotomy, trichotomy, and conditional unity. Monism asserts that humans are not composed of parts but are indivisible. This, the prevalent view of modern science, holds that one must have a body to be human. Monism rejects a disembodied existence in an intermediate state. Dichotomy asserts that humans are made up of two parts: a material one (the body) and an immaterial one (the soul or spirit). At death, body and soul separate. The body dies and the soul enters an intermediate state: God's presence for believers, hell for unbelievers. Trichotomy asserts that humans are made up of three parts: a body, a soul (the site of emotions and will), and a spirit (the site of contact with God). It agrees with dichotomy in affirming an intermediate state after death but holds that only the spirit goes there. Psychosomatic unity (also called conditional unity) asserts that normally body and soul are united. This unity is altered at death, where the immaterial part lives on while the material part decomposes. This disembodied intermediate state is abnormal and temporary, for in the resurrection God will unify people again. Scripture refutes the monistic view (Luke 23:43, 46; Phil 1:23; 2 Cor 5:6, 8). Human nature is not such a unity that a disembodied existence is impossible. Such an existence becomes actual in the intermediate state. Yet, if we view death in light of the Bible's story, then the intermediate existence is an anomaly, for God created Adam and Eve as embodied beings; we are embodied now; and after the resurrection we will live as embodied beings for all eternity. Indeed, our final state is not a disembodied existence; our final state will be in glorified bodies on the new earth. *See also* creation; image of God (*imago Dei*).

humanity, origin—the source of mankind's existence, typically explained by evolution or creation. Evolution holds that humans evolved from primates, while creationism holds that we are special creations of God. There are three understandings of evolution. Naturalistic evolution asserts that natural processes are responsible for everything that exists, including humans. This view is anti-supernaturalistic, leaving no place for God. Deistic evolution holds that God used evolution to achieve his ends. After creating the first form, God removed himself from the process. Theistic evolution is similar to, yet differs from, deistic evolution. It holds that God participates both in the beginning and at key points within the process. It teaches that God directly and supernaturally created human beings by imparting a human soul into a higher primate. The first two views flatly contradict biblical teaching. Evangelicals have held theistic evolution, though it does not seem to do justice to the biblical account of God's special creation of Adam and Eve. Creationism consists of two main positions. Fiat (or young earth) creationism holds that God, by a direct act, created everything immediately. It emphasizes both the directness of God's action and creation's short duration. Progressive (or old earth) creationism holds that God used a long process punctuated by points in time at which God created new creatures without using previously existing life. Between these special acts of creation, development occurred over long periods of time. Both progressive creationists and fiat creationists agree that God created humans directly and did not use a previously existing primate. *See also* creation; image of God (*imago Dei*).

humanity, states—stages of human existence, divided into the present state, the intermediate state, and the eternal state. The present state is life in the body. This is the normal state of affairs ever since God created Adam and Eve with body and soul united (1 Thess 5:23). The intermediate state is the state of human beings after death and before resurrection (Phil 1:23; 2 Cor 5:6–8). This state is abnormal and temporary because the soul is separated from the body. The final state is as resurrected beings with body and soul together again (Phil 3:20–21; 1 Cor 15:22). Believers will live like this forever on the new earth (Rev 21:1–4), and unbelievers will be resurrected and sent to hell (Dan 12:2; Matt 10:28). *See also* humanity, makeup; intermediate state; new heavens and new earth; resurrection.

humanity of Christ—*See* Christ's humanity; Christ's humanity, denials.

humiliation of Christ—*See* Christ's states of humiliation and exaltation.

humility—*See* virtues, Christian.

hyper-Calvinism—a position that overemphasizes God's sovereignty and minimizes human responsibility. It denies the universal and indiscriminate call of the gospel to the lost, and most Calvinists rightly reject it. *See also* Calvinism; Great Commission.

hypostatic union—*See* Christ's unity.

Ii

idealism—a monistic philosophy that holds that reality is fundamentally mental and immaterial. It holds that everything is composed of mind or spirit. Idealism thus stands in opposition to materialism, which teaches that all that exists is matter. Immanuel Kant and Georg Wilhelm Hegel were important idealists who dominated nineteenth-century philosophy. Early in the twentieth century, G. E. Moore and Bertrand Russell successfully attacked idealism, putting it out of favor for 100 years. *See also* analytic philosophy; dualism; empiricism; existentialism; materialism; monism; rationalism; skepticism.

idolatry—worship of anyone or anything other than the true God as if it were God. Idolatry is condemned in both Testaments (Exod 20:4–5; Rom 1:22–23). First John 5:21 warns Christians of committing idolatry in the heart by putting anything in God's place. *See also* greatness of God; Holy Spirit's works; Satan and demons; Ten Commandments; truthfulness of God; worship.

illumination—the work of the Holy Spirit to enable people to understand, believe, and apply Scripture. The same Spirit who inspired the Word of God works in hearers and readers of the Word so that they embrace its message. The Spirit works through Scripture to facilitate comprehension of the Bible, bring people to Christ, and motivate them to obey him (1 Cor 2:14–15). *See also* Holy Spirit's ministries; Scripture.

illumination theory of inspiration—*See* inspiration; inspiration, views.

image of God (*imago Dei*)—God's creating Adam and Eve so they would be like him in some way. Three views have prevailed in church history regarding this image or likeness (which are synonyms). *Substantive* or *structural* views reigned until the Enlightenment. Such views understand the image to be located in our makeup as humans, rather than in roles or relationships. Proponents point to reason as separating us from animals. The *functional* view of the image is more recent. It sees the image of God as consisting in our roles, not in our being. Advocates point to God's giving Adam and Eve dominion over the other creatures. As we likewise exercise dominion, we image God. The *relational* view of the image is also recent. It says that the image of God is found in our relationships, not in our being or roles. We image God in relating to him, fellow humans, and creation. This view sees love as the image's chief expression. In sum, there are five key aspects of the image. First, the image has substantive, functional, and relational aspects. God created Adam and Eve to be like him in their makeup. He made them righteous and with cognition to do his will (Eph 4:22–24; Col 3:9–10). God also gave Adam and Eve dominion over creation (Gen 1:26–28). They were also to relate to God, their fellow humans, and creation in ways that pleased God. Second, Jesus substantively is the image of God, and in his incarnation he perfectly models God's image (2 Cor 4:4; Col 1:15). Jesus is also the final goal for his people, who will one day be conformed to his image in immortality and glory (Rom 8:29; 1 Cor 15:49). Third, at creation God made Adam and Eve in his original image. After the fall, the image was marred but not erased (Gen 9:6; James 3:9). When people come to Christ, God begins a lifelong process of restoring them in his image (Col 3:10). Only in the eternal state will the image be perfected (1 Cor 15:49). Fourth, the image encompasses relationships to God, fellow human beings, and creation. Fifth, God created Adam and Eve in his image as holistic beings, made of bodies and souls. The perfected image will involve resurrected human beings, united in body and soul, serving the Trinity on the new earth. *See also* Christ as image of God.

immanence of God—*See* omnipresence of God.

immediate imputation—*See* imputation.

immersion—*See* baptism, mode.

imminence of the Second Coming—*See* Second Coming.

immortality—the ability to live forever and to be incapable of dying. Only God is inherently immortal (1 Tim 6:15–16). He is eternal, without beginning or end. God graciously gives immortality to human beings, and although we have a beginning, we have no end. Our immaterial part (our soul or spirit) survives the death of the body. God will raise all human beings from the dead on the last day, and all will exist forever. Scripture implies immortality when it teaches the eternity of punishment for the wicked and of life for the righteous: "They will go away into eternal punishment, but the righteous into eternal life" (Matt 25:46). Scripture does not use the phrase "immortality of the soul" but ascribes immortality to our resurrected bodies (1 Cor 15:53). *See also* eternity of God; glorification; heaven; hell; resurrection.

immutability of God—God's inability to change in his character or nature. Unlike his changing creation, he is stable (Jas 1:17). God's unchangeableness gives us great security (Ps 102:27–28; Mal 3:6). While his character remains constant, he is also a personal Being who enters into covenant with his people. *See also* faithfulness of God.

impassibility of God—the reality that God's experiences do not come upon him as ours come upon us. We are often surprised by what we encounter, but God is not. What he experiences is within his sovereignty and foreknowledge. Nothing outside of God causes him to change in his nature, knowledge, or will. He cannot be influenced to be unfaithful or to default on his promises. God is not swayed by temptation or sin. But this does not mean that he lacks emotions or does not care about humans and their suffering. He loves righteousness and hates sin (Ps 45:7). He loves a world that hates him, and he sent his Son to save it (John 3:16). That God is both impassible and caring is difficult to understand because it is a subcategory of the fact that he is infinite and personal. *See also* anthropomorphism; anthropopathism; love of God; spirituality of God.

impeccability—the inability of the incarnate Son of God to sin while on earth. The eternal Son could not sin before his incarnation, and he cannot sin now in heaven. Evangelicals debate whether he could have sinned while on earth. Some hold to peccability, the view that it was possible for Christ to sin, saying that otherwise his temptations would not have been real. Most evangelicals hold to impeccability and say that his divine nature prevented him from sinning. Most important, all agree that he had no sin nature and never sinned (2 Cor 5:21; 1 John 3:5). All also agree that he successfully endured real temptations (Luke 4:1–2; Heb 4:15). *See also* Christ's incarnation; Christ's states of humiliation and exaltation; sin.

imputation—the legal crediting or charging of something to someone. Scripture describes three imputations. The imputation of Adam's original sin causes all humans to be guilty before God and morally polluted (immediate imputation). The imputation of our sins to Christ on the cross explains how he could die for our sins, taking our place. The imputation of Christ's righteousness to us when we believe the gospel is the basis of God's declaring us righteous in Christ (justification) (Rom 4:3–5; 5:18–19; 2 Cor 5:21; Gal 3:13). *See also* justification; sin.

in Christ—*See* union with Christ.

inability—*See* fall, the; free will; total depravity.

incarnation—*See* Christ's incarnation.

inclusivism—*See* exclusivism/inclusivism/pluralism.

incommunicable attributes of God—characteristics of God that are unique to him and that he does not share with human beings. These include aseity, unity, spirituality (God is a spiritual being and has no body), infinity, omnipresence, omnipotence, omniscience, eternity, immutability, and greatness. *See also* attributes of God; communicable attributes of God.

incompatibilism—the view that absolute divine sovereignty and genuine human freedom are inconsistent. It holds that God's absolute sovereignty would destroy human moral responsibility. For this reason, incompatibilism affirms libertarian freedom, the idea that humans are the ultimate cause of their actions and that not even God overrides this freedom. Incompatibilism therefore limits God's sovereignty to make room for human free will. Although we cannot fully understand, Scripture teaches both divine sovereignty and human responsibility. *See also* compatibilism; free will; sovereignty of God.

indwelling of the Spirit—*See* Holy Spirit's deity; Holy Spirit's ministries.

indwelling sin—the presence and activity of sin in believers' lives. Since the fall, sin is a universal aspect of the human condition. It is also an inherent condition. Every human being is born with a sinful nature, a tendency for evil that is the source of actual sins. Although this truth is implied in other scriptures, Paul explicitly teaches that sin continues to live in every Christian. In a passage in which he struggles with sin overwhelming his desire to do good, Paul speaks of "sin living in [him]" and of "the sin that lives in [him]" and says that "evil is present with [him]" (Rom 7:17, 20–21). Although indwelling sin is not an excuse for believers to give themselves over to a sinful lifestyle, sin will unfortunately be in and with us until Christ returns to confirm us in perfect holiness. It is no wonder that early Christians cried out, "Our Lord, come!" (1 Cor 16:22) and "Come, Lord Jesus!" (Rev 22:20). *See also* sin; sin nature.

inerrancy—the quality of Scripture as being without error (inerrant) and truthful in all that it affirms, grounded in the fact that God inspired the Bible (2 Tim 3:16–17). Biblically, truth includes fidelity, factual accuracy, and completeness. Because the persons of the Trinity are true and speak only truth (Father, John 3:33; Son, 14:6; Holy Spirit, 16:13), Scripture is true in all three senses. Fidelity: Scripture is true, as God faithfully reveals himself and his will in the Bible (Ps 145:13; Rev 21:5). Factual accuracy: Scripture is truthful, for it corresponds to factual and spiritual reality (Ps 119:160; 2 Tim 2:15). Completeness: Scripture is truth in its completeness, for in it God supplies all believers' needs for eternal life and holiness (2 Pet 1:3–4). God speaks truth in his Word to save and sanctify his people. While meeting those goals, Scripture speaks truthfully on all matters it touches, including those concerning history or science. Inerrancy is the historic view of the church. *See also* Chicago Statement on Biblical Inerrancy; Henry, Carl F. H.; inspiration; inspiration, views; Scripture, attributes; truth.

infallibility—the quality of Scripture as being incapable of error. Historically synonymous with "inerrant." Scripture will not fail to accomplish its purpose—God's Word does not err and is reliable to lead people to salvation and equip them in Christian living. More recently, some have used "infallible" to claim that the Bible is not inerrant but will nevertheless accomplish its purpose. This is an erroneous view (Isa 55:10–11; Rom 1:16; 10:17; 2 Tim 3:16–17; Heb 4:12–13). *See also* inerrancy; inspiration; inspiration, views; Scripture, attributes; truth.

infant baptism (pedobaptism)—the practice of baptizing the babies of Christian parents. Proponents point to continuity between the Testaments. God commanded that male infants be circumcised in the Abrahamic covenant, and since the new covenant is its fulfillment, babies should receive baptism, the sign of entrance into the new covenant. Roman Catholic, Lutheran, and Reformed churches baptize infants and adults, while Baptists baptize only believers. The first two of these denominations hold to baptismal regeneration, the view that baptism saves those baptized, while the latter two do not. Reformed churches hold that by baptism God welcomes people, including infants, into the visible church. Baptism is viewed as a sign and seal of union with Christ, regeneration, forgiveness, and of dedication to God but not as necessary for salvation. Baptists reject infant baptism because there is no clear example of it in the New Testament, where those baptized are believers. *See also* baptism, views; baptismal regeneration; believer's baptism.

infinity of God—God's attribute of being unlimited in his person and attributes. His infinity with regard to time is his eternity. His infinity with regard to space is his omnipresence. His infinity with regard to power is his omnipotence. His infinity with regard to knowledge is his omniscience (Isa 40:28; Ps 147:5; Eph 1:18–19). *See also* attributes of God; eternity of God; omnipotence of God; omnipresence of God; omniscience of God.

inheritance—*See* adoption.

inner witness of the Holy Spirit—*See* assurance of salvation.

inspiration—the supernatural action of God working through human authors to produce Scripture as a revelation of himself. God inspired the biblical writers and their writings (2 Tim 3:15–17). All Scripture is "God-breathed" (v. 16 NIV), spoken forth by God. He worked by his Spirit through humans to produce the very Word of God (Ps 19:7–11; 2 Tim 3:15) in human language (2 Pet 1:20–21). Inspired by God, Scripture is truthful (inerrant, Ps 119:160; John 17:17; 2 Tim 2:15), authoritative (2 Tim 3:15–4:5; 2 Pet 1:19), sufficient (Luke 16:29–31; 2 Pet 1:3–4, 19), clear (Neh 8:1–12; Acts 17:11–12), and is a key way God acts to accomplish his mission to glorify himself through faith in Jesus (Isa 55:10–11; Rom 1:16; 10:17). Inspiration is dynamic, as God actively works through active human authors. It is also verbal, referring to the prophets' actual words (not only ideas) and writings (2 Tim 3:15–17). And it is plenary (full), for "*All* Scripture is inspired by God," not merely its parts (2 Tim 3:16). *See also* concurrence; inspiration, views; Scripture; Scripture, attributes; truth; truthfulness of God.

inspiration, views—various explanations for the way God inspired Holy Scripture. The *intuition theory* holds that inspiration is a matter of insight exercised by religious geniuses with great spiritual awareness. To the contrary, inspiration is a special work of God, speaking his Word through the Scripture writers. The Spirit directed the writers so that they spoke *for God* (2 Pet 1:21). The *illumination theory* holds that the Holy Spirit works in all believers; he worked in the Scripture writers to a greater degree, heightening their normal powers. To the contrary, the inspiration of Scripture is different in kind, not only in degree, from other types of "inspiration." Every Scripture passage is the result of God's speaking forth his Word (2 Tim 3:16). The *dynamic theory* holds that God worked with human writers to produce Scripture. The Spirit guided them to have the thoughts that he wanted, which they expressed in their own words. This theory correctly sees God and humans as working together to create Scripture. God used the writers' styles, vocabularies, and so forth, to express his Word. But this theory errs when it limits God's influence to the thoughts of Scripture. He also spoke forth the words (2 Tim 3:16). The *verbal theory* holds that the Holy Spirit gave the writers not only the thoughts but also the words, so that Scripture contains the very words God wanted written. This differs from the dictation theory, because here human authors were active. This theory is correct in what it affirms but is incomplete. It does not sufficiently assert the divine-human working together of the dynamic theory. The *dictation theory* holds that God dictated Scripture's very words and the writers were largely passive. This theory rightly affirms that the words of Scripture are God's words, but it incorrectly holds dictation as the mode of inspiration. Although God dictated parts of Scripture, the different styles and vocabularies of the writers (e.g., Luke 1:1–4) will not allow for dictation of the whole. Instead, God authored the Bible using human writers. The *neoorthodox view* claims that orthodoxy holds to divine dictation of Scripture. Revelation consists of God himself, not in propositions about him but in his acts in Israel's history and in Jesus. Revelation is subjective, and without appropriation no revelation occurs. This view rightly affirms the importance of God's personal revelation. But it errs in four ways. First, it caricatures orthodoxy. Evangelicals reject the dictation theory, adopting instead an organic view in which God and human authors both played roles. Second, it denies that personal revelation occurred in words. Third, God reveals himself in deed *and* word. Because deeds are not self-interpreting, God speaks to interpret his acts. Fourth, though people do not benefit spiritually from God's truth without faith, revelation occurs whether or not they appropriate it. *Limited inerrancy* opposes full inerrancy. Scripture is inerrant in what pertains to faith and life but not necessarily in matters of history, science, and other disciplines. This view rightly denies that the Bible is a history or science text. Its advocates err, however, when they teach that Scripture stumbles in matters of history, science, and so on. God speaks truth in his Word. Its purposes are to save and sanctify his people. In writing to accomplish those goals, God speaks truthfully of other matters as well. The Bible does not speak with modern scientific precision, but it speaks truth. Some holding to limited inerrancy deny inerrancy but hold to infallibility, which they define as Scripture unfailingly accomplishing God's purposes. This misuses the word "infallibility" to teach errancy. Scripture uses various literary genres to accomplish God's many purposes, but it does so inerrantly. The biblical concept of truth involves not only faithfulness but also factualness and completeness. Those adopting full inerrancy hold to the complete truthfulness of the Bible without denying its infallibility. The orthodox view of inspiration holds that God worked supernaturally with the writers of Scripture so that their words are fully (plenary) inspired (verbal) to produce the very Word of God written and to accomplish dynamically all that God intends, including speaking truth (inerrancy). *See also* concurrence; inerrancy; inspiration; Scripture; Scripture, attributes.

intercession—*See* prayer; worship.

intercession of Christ—*See* Christ's saving work.

intermediate state—the situation of human beings after death and before resurrection. The normal state of affairs is for body and soul to be united. That is how God created us, how we live now, and how we will live forever after the resurrection. Death is separation, and physical death temporarily and abnormally separates our material and immaterial parts. God will reunite our bodies and souls in the resurrection. At death believers' bodies are put in graves, but our immaterial parts go immediately into Christ's presence (Luke 23:43; 2 Cor 5:6–8; Phil 1:21–24). Scripture teaches that the unsaved (those who reject Christ as Lord and Savior) will experience an intermediate hell, where the soul goes after separation from the body at death (Luke 16:22–25; 2 Pet 2:9–10). Two errors associated with the intermediate state are soul sleep and purgatory. Soul sleep is the teaching that at death a person's soul "sleeps"—is inert and unconscious—until the resurrection. To the contrary, Scripture teaches that at death believers are with Jesus in paradise, that to die is gain (Phil 1:21), and that to be "away from the body" is to be "at home with the Lord" (2 Cor 5:8). Roman Catholic doctrine views purgatory as a place where the venial sins of the faithful Catholics (not everyone) are cleansed (purged) after death until they are ready for heaven. The Reformers rightly viewed purgatory as an insult to Christ's death, which purchased salvation for all believers (Heb 10:10; 13:12). Believers' sins do not need purging at death. Rather, because of Christ's work, God will "sanctify" us "completely." He will keep us "sound and blameless at the coming of our Lord Jesus Christ." We can be sure of this, for "he who calls [us] is faithful; he will do it" (1 Thess 5:23–24). *See also* creation; humanity, makeup; image of God (*imago Dei*).

internal call—*See* calling.

interpretation of Scripture—*See* hermeneutics.

intersectionality—a term originating in black feminist theory, that has become a framework for analyzing various forms of social stratification that can cause discrimination. It highlights how power and social categories (ethnicity, class, gender, age, etc.) interrelate and affect the treatment of individuals and groups. Positively, aspects of the theory can help Christians better understand those marginalized, address personal and structural sin, and promote thoughtful social justice. However, negatively, the theory of intersectionality is usually associated with proponents of relativism and liberation theology, who oppose Christian perspectives on truth, identity, gender, sexuality, and more. *See also* liberation theology; relativism.

intuition theory of inspiration—*See* inspiration; inspiration, views.

invisible church—*See* church.

Irenaeus (c. 130–c. 200)—principal Christian theologian of the second century who opposed Gnosticism in *Against Heresies* (c. 180). By attacking Gnostic works claiming to be Scripture, he helped to establish the biblical canon. When Gnostics rejected the Old Testament, he asserted the validity of both Testaments. When Gnostics claimed a secret oral tradition from Jesus, Irenaeus held that no bishops were Gnostics. Because Gnostics denied that the God of the New Testament was the Creator, the Apostles' Creed began with that truth. Irenaeus famously presented Christ's work as a recapitulation, in which he restored through obedience what Adam had lost through disobedience. *See also* Apostles' Creed; canon; Christ's saving work.

irresistible grace—*See* Calvinism.

Israel—*See* dispensationalism; millennium; new covenant.

Jj

Jesus—*See* Christ's names and titles.

Jesus Christ—*See* Christ's person and work; Trinity.

Jesus as King—*See* Christ's offices.

Jesus as Mediator of the new covenant—*See* mediator; new covenant.

Jesus as priest—*See* Christ's offices.

Jesus as prophet—*See* Christ's offices.

Jerusalem, destruction of—*See* signs of the times.

joy—*See* virtues, Christian.

judgment—*See* hell; Last Judgment.

justice—God's requirement that we deal righteously (justly) with one another, in light of his own righteous dealings with humans. Human justice is best understood in light of God's. He governs the world morally and treats his creatures justly. He cares for the poor and downtrodden. God is a just Judge, and, remarkably, his righteousness also brings salvation in Christ. Jesus regarded human justice as a very important matter of the law (Matt 23:23). This involves humans giving their fellows what is rightfully theirs. This means rewarding those who follow the law and penalizing those who do not. This includes caring for the poor and freeing those oppressed. *See also* righteousness (justice) of God.

justice of God—*See* righteousness (justice) of God.

justification—God's declaring righteous those sinners who believe in Christ. Justification is by God's grace alone, through faith alone, in Christ alone. We all need justification because we are guilty before a holy God and cannot rescue ourselves. God in his grace is the source of our justification. The basis for his declaring sinners righteous is Jesus's death and resurrection. Jesus's death accomplishes both expiation, the removal of sin (Heb 9:26), and propitiation, the removal of wrath (Rom 3:25–26). The cross turns away God's judgment as Christ dies as a propitiation, taking the wrath that our sins deserve. Justification is a declaration of righteousness rather than an infusion of righteousness, as the Roman Catholic Church teaches. It involves the imputation of Christ's righteousness to believers (2 Cor 5:21). Christ's righteousness is alien righteousness, the righteousness of another outside of us credited to us. Justification is also defined biblically as the non-imputation of sin, bringing forgiveness (Rom 4:6–8). The means of justification is faith, not works. Although God works in the lives of his people to produce holiness, this is never the basis of his acceptance of them. Therefore, they are *simul justus et peccator*, at the same time righteous in Christ but sinners in themselves (Rom 3:10–12; 4:1–8; 5:18–19; Gal 2:16). *See also* application of salvation; imputation; Luther, Martin; propitiation; Reformation; Roman Catholicism.

Justin Martyr (c. 100–c. 165)—eminent Christian apologist who defended the Christian faith against pagan attacks. After finding pagan philosophies unfulfilling, he became a Christian in 132. As a Christian philosopher, he wrote two *Apologies* and the *Dialogue with Trypho* (a Jew with whom Justin debates biblical interpretation), seeking to reconcile Christian faith and reason. Jesus is the incarnation of the whole divine Logos and basic truths, while only bits of these truths appear in the best philosophers' writings. Justin's *Apologies* argue that Christianity does not threaten Rome and is superior to paganism. Justin was arrested and beheaded when he refused to offer incense to the emperor, for which he is called Martyr. *See also* apologetics.

Kant, Immanuel (1724–1804)—German thinker who impacted all subsequent philosophy. As a father of the Enlightenment, he urged people to think uninhibited by any external authority. Kant placed humans as active knowers at the center of knowledge and morality. His *Critique of Pure Reason* (1781) affected all later epistemology. He taught that human minds do not know things as they are in themselves but apprehend them through the senses. In this process, minds shape and structure experience. His *Critique of Practical Reason* presented reason as the source of morality. The basis for ethics, he believed, is in the natural human will following intrinsically valid principles and not in any other authority, including God. Kant promoted agnosticism, for we cannot know with certainty whether there is a God or an afterlife. *See also* epistemology; ethics; modernism; postmodernism.

kenosis doctrine—*See* Christ's deity; Christ's deity, denials.

Kierkegaard, Søren (1813–1855)—Danish theologian, social critic, psychologist, and the first existentialist philosopher. He emphasized the actual human life of the individual over abstract thinking. He wrote on the infinite distance separating God and humans and on the emotions—especially angst and despair—of people facing hard choices. He stressed the believer's subjective relationship to God and Christian love. To have Christian faith means making a leap, committing oneself totally to God despite lacking objective proofs for the truth of Christianity. He vigorously attacked the state church of Denmark as hypocritical and lacking compassion. Among his writings are more than 7,000 pages of journals, *Fear and Trembling*, and *Philosophical Fragments*. *See also* epistemology; existentialism; faith.

King, Martin Luther, Jr. (1929–1968)—the leading figure in the American civil rights movement. After seminary, he became the first African American to earn a PhD in theology and was ordained an American Baptist minister. In December 1955, he led the first African American non-violent protest in a bus boycott in Montgomery, Alabama, after Rosa Parks refused to give up her seat to a white man. This event led the Supreme Court to declare unconstitutional laws that required segregated buses. King was elected president of the Southern Christian Leadership Conference in 1957. Taking ideals from Christianity and methods from Gandhi, between 1957–68 he traveled 6,000 miles, spoke 2,500 times, and wrote four books. He also led a massive protest in Birmingham, Alabama, was arrested, and wrote "Letter from a Birmingham Jail," a manifesto of the civil rights movement. He led a peaceful march of 250,000 on Washington, DC, where he gave his famous "I Have a Dream" speech. He became the youngest, at age thirty-five, to be awarded the Nobel Peace Prize (1964). King was assassinated on April 4, 1968.

kingdom of God—God's reign over his people. God's kingdom is present and future; it is "already" and "not yet." He reigns in the present age and will reign more fully in the age to come. The Old Testament teaches God's *universal* rule (Ps 103:19) over angels and humans of all nations (Dan 4:34–35). It also teaches his *particular* rule over his people Israel, including promises of an eternal kingdom to David and his descendants, including the Messiah (2 Sam 7:12–16; Isa 9:6–7). God's kingdom comes with newness and power in the New Testament. It is inaugurated by Jesus the Messiah, expands in his exaltation, and will be consummated at his return. Jesus is the King whose words (Matt 4:17) and deeds, especially casting out demons, bring the spiritual kingdom of God (12:28). In his ascension Jesus moves from the limited earthly sphere to the transcendent heavenly one. He sits at God's right hand, the place of highest honor and authority (Eph 1:20–21). Jesus pours out the Spirit on the church at Pentecost, mightily expanding God's kingdom as thousands come to Christ (Acts 2:41; 4:4; 5:31). The fullness of the kingdom awaits Jesus's return to sit "on his glorious throne" (Matt 25:31). He will judge the world, allowing believers to "inherit the kingdom" while consigning the lost to eternal punishment (25:31–46). In the end God will rule over the new heavens and new earth (Rev 20:11; 21:1). *See also* "already" and "not yet"; Christ's offices; heaven; new heavens and new earth.

Knox, John (c. 1514–1572)—principal leader of the Scottish Reformation. Scots opposed the Roman Catholic Church because of its wealth and its clergy's immorality. Knox reluctantly accepted a call to preach when the Catholic Church persecuted Protestantism, and he became a galley slave for over a year. Released, he developed his theological understanding in Calvin's Geneva. Back in Scotland, he was a powerful preacher who inspired riots against the Catholic Church. When Protestantism became accepted in Scotland, Knox and others wrote a Calvinistic and Presbyterian Confession of Faith. Along with controversial writings, his most significant work was the *History of the Reformation in Scotland*. *See also* Calvin, John; Reformation.

lake of fire—*See* hell.

Lamb of God—*See* Christ's names and titles.

last days—the time between Christ's first and second comings. Old Testament prophets foretold the last days (Isa 2:2; Hos 3:5; Mic 4:1). The New Testament announces that the last days have arrived in the coming of Christ (Heb 1:2), the day of Pentecost (Acts 2:16–17), and the appearance of people who scoff at the idea of Christ's second coming (2 Pet 3:3–4). Indeed, the New Testament age is the fulfillment of the Old Testament hope (1 Cor 10:11; Heb 9:26). Christ brought the last days with his first coming and will bring them to a close with his return. *See also* prophecy; Second Coming.

Last Judgment—God's assigning people to their eternal destinies. "It is a terrifying thing to fall into the hands of the living God" (Heb 10:31) and stand before the One who sits on "a great white throne" of judgment, for "earth and heaven fled from his presence, and no place was found for them" (Rev 20:11–12). Every human being is accountable to God (Rom 3:19). The Last Judgment will occur at the end of the age (Matt 13:40–43), after Jesus returns (25:31–32, 46)—after the resurrection of the dead (Rev 20:12–13) and before the new heavens and new earth (2 Pet 3:7, 13). The chief purpose of the Last Judgment is to display God's glory manifested in his sovereignty (Rev 11:17–18), righteousness (16:5–6), power (11:17–18), truth (15:3), and holiness (15:4). Another purpose is to assign, not to determine, eternal destinies (Matt 25:34, 41; John 5:28–29). Another purpose is to reveal degrees of reward (Luke 19:17–19; 1 Cor 3:14–15) and punishment (Matt 11:21–24; Luke 12:47–48; Rom 2:5). The elements of the

Last Judgment include the Judge, those who are judged, and the judgment itself. Scripture sometimes presents the Father (1 Pet 1:17; Rev 20:11) and sometimes the Son as the Judge at the Last Judgment (John 5:22; Acts 17:31). God will judge evil angels (Matt 25:41; Jude v. 6; Rev 20:10) and human beings (Rom 3:5–6; Rev 20:12–15). He will judge the latter justly based on thoughts (1 Cor 4:5), words (Matt 12:36), and deeds (2 Cor 5:10; Rev 20:13). Importantly, judgment based on works does not threaten salvation by grace, for judgment reveals if salvation is present. The saved pass the judgment, but the lost do not (Eph 2:10; Titus 3:8; Jas 2:18). *See also* grace of God; hell; preterism; Second Coming; wrath of God.

last things—*See* eschatology.

law—The term *law* is from the Hebrew word *torah*, which can be translated "instruction" and can refer to a broad range of topics, from the Ten Commandments, moral laws, civil laws, and ceremonial laws to the Word of God itself. *See* law, uses.

law, uses—ways that God uses his law, or moral instruction, in the world. From the Reformation, Protestants have recognized three uses of the law (summarized in the Ten Commandments). First, in its condemnatory use, the law is a good instrument to show sinners how far they fall short of God's glory and therefore need Christ. Second, in the civil use, the second table of the law (commandments five through ten) plays an important role in the legal code of nations, prohibiting murder and theft, for example. Third, in its Christian use, the law is a prod and guide for the Christian life. *See also* antinomianism; law; legalism; sanctification; spirituality; spiritual disciplines; Ten Commandments.

legalism—(1) The view that salvation is merited by keeping the law. A merit theology holds that obedience to the law gains God's favor and earns eternal life. Jesus combated the legalism of the Pharisees (John 5:39–40, 45) and Paul the legalism of the Judaizers (Gal 2:15–16). Jesus condemned self-righteous legalism and extolled God's mercy for sinners (Luke 18:9–14). Paul condemned legalism and extolled God's saving grace (Rom 3:28; Eph 2:8–9). (2) The view that the essence of the Christian life is law keeping. Antinomianism errs in the opposite manner when it denies that believers need the law. God's law as a part of God's Word has a place in the Christian life, for believers show their love for God by obeying him. But grace, faith, the Holy Spirit, and freedom in Christ occupy pride of place in the life of the church, as well as that of individual Christians. *See also* antinomianism; asceticism; law; law, uses; sanctification; Ten Commandments.

Levitical priesthood—*See* Christ's offices.

Lewis, C. S. (1898–1963)—British professor of English literature, author of popular fiction, and foremost Christian apologist of the twentieth century. *See also* apologetics.

liberalism (theological, not political)—a nineteenth- and twentieth-century dismissal of historic Christian theology seeking freedom from external controls and adjusting to modern thought and culture. Friedrich Schleiermacher, regarded as its founder, wrote the influential systematic theology *The Christian Faith*, attempting to reconcile Enlightenment ideas with Christianity. Liberalism downplayed the supernatural and sought to modernize the faith to make it believable and helpful to modern people. Liberalism emphasizes action, not belief, and life, not doctrine. *See also* doctrine; ecumenism; evangelicalism; modernism; neoorthodoxy; truth.

liberation theology—a movement, beginning in the mid-twentieth century, that sought to fuse Christian theology and Marxism. Varieties included black, feminist, and Third-World theologies. Citing scriptures treating liberation and God's concern for the poor, liberation theology identified with the poor and sought political liberation for the oppressed. Leading Latin American exponents included Gustavo Gutiérrez of Peru, Leonardo Boff of Brazil, and Juan Luis Segundo of Uruguay. Radical liberation theologies taught sin as oppression; God as being on the side of the oppressed; and salvation as freedom from oppression, even to the point of violence. Evangelicals such as René Padilla of Ecuador, Samuel Escobar of Peru, and Orlando E. Costas of Puerto Rico spurned radical liberation theology, instead uniting evangelism and social responsibility to aid the oppressed, poor, and marginalized. *See also* Christ's saving work, biblical images; Cone, James; evangelism; Great Commission; Gutiérrez, Gustavo; Padilla, René; poor, the.

libertarian freedom—*See* compatibilism; free will; incompatibilism.

likeness—*See* image of God (*imago Dei*).

limited atonement—*See* Calvinism.

limited inerrancy—*See* inspiration, views.

liturgy—a Christian church's form of public worship. *See also* worship.

living God—*See* aseity of God.

logic—the study of correct reasoning, focusing on the drawing of inferences. An inference is a step, governed by rules, from one or more propositions, called premises, to a conclusion. One of the four main branches of philosophy. *See also* epistemology; ethics; metaphysics.

long-suffering of God—*See* patience of God.

Lord of Armies ("of Hosts")—*See* God, names of.

Lord Jesus—*See* titles of Christ.

Lord's Prayer—Jesus's famous model prayer in Matt 6:9–13, comprising six petitions. First, we are to pray that God's person would be honored as holy. Second, we are to pray for the coming of God's kingdom. Third, closely related to the second petition, we are to pray that the Father's "will be done on earth as it is in heaven" (vv. 10–11). Fourth, we are to request daily bread from our Father's hand. Fifth, we are to pray to be forgiven as we forgive others (v. 12). Sixth, we are to ask our Father not to lead us into those places where we would stumble and fall spiritually. Instead, we are to seek God's deliverance from the devil and evil. This simple prayer thus covers the key areas of life: glorifying God, his kingdom coming, doing his will, our daily provision, ongoing forgiveness, and victory over evil. These are aspects of our Father's love for us and ways we can honor him as we live on earth, with the knowledge that he is our Father in heaven. *See also* prayer; sanctification; temptation; worship.

Lord's Supper—the Christian ordinance of remembrance of Christ's death and communion with him and one another. Besides baptism, Jesus gave his church the ordinance of the Lord's Supper. It looks back to Jesus's crucifixion and forward to his return, and in the present proclaims his death. On the new earth there will be no need for baptism or the Lord's Supper. The meal has a number of names. It is the Lord's Supper that he ordained, turning the Passover into a symbol of Christ's sacrifice (1 Cor 11:17–34). It is a Eucharist, or thanksgiving (v. 24). It is a Communion, an invigoration of union with Christ (10:16). The theology of the Lord's Supper is rich. First, it is an ordinance commanded by Jesus (Matt 26:26–28). Second, the Lord's Supper is a memorial that commemorates Jesus's death (1 Cor 11:23–25). Third, it is covenantal, for it points back to Jesus's sacrifice that ratified the new covenant (Luke 22:20). Fourth, the Lord's Supper unites the church. A communal meal, it displays our unity with Christ and one another (1 Cor 10:16–17). It calls us to show love and deference to one another (11:17–34). Fifth, the Supper heralds the gospel: "As often as you eat this bread and drink the cup, you proclaim the Lord's death until he comes" (1 Cor 11:26). Sixth, it praises Jesus's provision. It is a participation in the benefits of his saving work (1 Cor 10:14–22). We bring our sin to the Table and receive from God's abundant grace and Jesus's finished work. The Supper testifies to God's provision for us—grace upon grace. Seventh, the Lord's Supper predicts Jesus's return, as he promised (Matt 26:29) and as Paul reminds us (1 Cor 11:26). *See also* church, marks; gospel; Lord's Supper, views; ordinances or sacraments; Second Coming.

Lord's Supper, views—theological positions regarding the presence of Christ in the elements of Communion. Four such views have prevailed: Roman Catholic, Lutheran, Reformed, and Zwinglian. The Roman Catholic view is called transubstantiation. It holds that in ordination, priests receive the authority to offer Christ in the sacrifice of the mass. The Catholic Church teaches that when the priest consecrates the elements, they miraculously become the body and blood of Christ. Their outward appearance does not change, but miraculously the invisible essence of the elements changes into Christ's body and blood. The priest offers a non-bloody sacrifice of Christ to God in the mass. The Lutheran view of the Supper rejects Roman Catholic ideas of sacrifice and transubstantiation. Their view is called consubstantiation. The Supper is not a priestly sacrifice to God but a benefit that he bestows on worshippers. The elements do not change, but Christ is bodily present in, with, and under the elements. Lutherans hold that in Christ's resurrection his omnipresence was supernaturally transferred from his deity to his humanity. This enables his body to be everywhere present, including in the elements of Communion. The Reformed view of the Lord's Supper differs from both Roman Catholic and Lutheran views. It is sometimes called the doctrine of Christ's real presence. It rejects both transubstantiation and consubstantiation. The elements do not change, and Christ's body is in heaven. This view holds that Christ is present in the Supper as the Holy Spirit brings the benefits of Christ from his place at the Father's right hand to believing participants. The Zwinglian view of the Supper differs from the others. Although it is debatable whether it was the view of Ulrich Zwingli, it remains attached to his name. It is called the memorial view, for it emphasizes the church's remembering Jesus in his death. The Supper is a commemoration that brings to mind Christ's atoning death. *See also* Calvin, John; church, marks; Lord's Supper; Luther, Martin; ordinances or sacraments; Reformation; Roman Catholicism; Zwingli, Ulrich.

lordship of Christ—(1) Jesus's right as crucified, risen Lord sitting at God's right hand to rule over all; (2) redeemed people's acknowledging Jesus's rule over their lives. Exalting Christ in his ascension and session, God proclaims him "both Lord and Messiah" (Acts 2:36). The primitive Christian response to salvation involves confessing Jesus as Lord and Savior (Rom 10:9). A day is coming when all will bow before Christ and acknowledge his lordship (Phil 2:11). In the meantime, his people gladly in their "hearts regard Christ the Lord as holy" and submit to him, who loved them and gave himself for them (1 Pet 3:15). *See also* Christ's names and titles; Christ's saving work; faith.

love—*See* fruit of the Spirit; virtues, Christian.

love of God—God's desiring others' good and his giving of himself to bring about that good. He cares deeply for humans (Exod 34:6–7), and, since we are rebels, his boundless love for us is undeserved (Ps 103:10–11; Rom 5:8). God's love is great and everlasting; he even loves a world that hates him (Jer 31:3; John 3:16, 19–20). The Father, Son, and Holy Spirit love one another eternally (John 10:17; 14:31; 17:24). This trinitarian love reaches us as well (John 15:9; Rom 5:5; 1 John 4:10). God's love brings staggering privileges. He welcomes us into his family (1 John 3:1), removes our fear of final judgment (4:17), and assures us that nothing will separate us from his love in Christ (Rom 8:39). God's love also brings great responsibility. Jesus taught, "Just as I have loved you, you are also to love one another" (John 13:34). John adds that because God "loved us and sent his Son to be the propitiation for our sins . . . , we also ought to love one another" (1 John 4:10–11 ESV). *See also* adoption; assurance of salvation; grace of God; Holy Spirit's gifts; Trinity; virtues, Christian.

Luther, Martin (1483–1546)—professor of theology and preacher who questioned the Roman Catholic view on indulgences in his Ninety-Five Theses of 1517 and unwittingly sparked the Reformation. Luther came to oppose Catholic teaching by regarding Scripture more highly than the church and by holding that justification is received as a gift of God's grace alone through faith alone in Christ alone. Luther decreased the number of sacraments from seven to two: baptism and the Lord's Supper. His translation of the Bible into German impacted both the church and German culture. His hymns influenced the development of singing in Protestant churches. *See also* Calvin, John; Erasmus; faith; justification; Reformation; Roman Catholicism; *sola scriptura*; Zwingli, Ulrich.

Lutherans—Protestant Christians who trace their lineage to Martin Luther and the Reformation. Following Luther, they view Scripture as the highest religious authority and teach justification by grace, which means the imputation of Christ's righteousness to believing sinners. Lutherans baptize infants and hold to baptismal regeneration and the belief that Christ's body is in, with, and under the elements in the Lord's Supper. Lutheranism's foundational documents are the Augsburg Confession and the Formula of Concord (1530), which are contained with other documents in the *Book of Concord*. *See also* Augsburg Confession; Luther, Martin; Reformation.

Lutheran view of baptism—*See* baptism, views.

Lutheran view of Lord's Supper—*See* Lord's Supper, views.

Mm

Mary—a young, Jewish virgin whom God chose to give birth to his Son in his incarnation. Mary conceives through the Holy Spirit without Joseph's involvement (Matt 1:18, 20; Luke 1:35). She is blessed by God for her obedience and faith (v. 38), which make her an example to all. In her famous song of praise, Mary rejoices "in God [her] Savior" (v. 47). Roman Catholic dogma teaches that Mary was conceived without original sin, was perpetually a virgin, and did not die, but was assumed bodily into heaven. Evangelicals reject these claims as unbiblical. *See also* Christ's incarnation; Roman Catholicism.

materialism—the monistic philosophical view that the ultimate reality is matter, and nothing exists except matter and its interactions. Materialism thus rejects the reality of God, spirit, or consciousness. It stands in opposition to idealism, which teaches that all that exists is mind or spirit. *See also* agnosticism; apatheism; atheism; dualism; idealism; monism; naturalism.

means of grace—channels by which God conveys blessing and strength to believers. These traditionally include the preaching of the Word, observance of the ordinances (sacraments), and prayer. Some churches eschew the term *means of grace* to avoid confusion with Roman Catholicism's view that God gives infused grace through Rome's seven sacraments. *See also* church, marks; mysticism; ordinances or sacraments; prayer; preaching; Roman Catholicism.

mediator—one who goes between opposing parties to reconcile them. In Scripture, the "one mediator between God and humanity" is "the man

Christ Jesus" (1 Tim 2:5). We need a mediator because we rebel against God and provoke his holy anger. The mediator has to be God to bring about reconciliation. He also has to be a man to bridge the gap between holy God and sinners. In fulfillment of Old Testament promises of a new covenant, Jesus comes as Mediator of that new covenant and dies as Redeemer in the place of sinners. As a result of Jesus's mediation, God makes peace between himself and believers, who now have peace with God through Christ (John 14:6; Heb 8:6; 9:15; 12:24). *See also* Christ's deity; Christ's humanity; Christ's saving work, biblical images; new covenant.

meditation—*See* spiritual disciplines.

memorial view of Communion—*See* Lord's Supper; Lord's Supper, views.

mercy of God—God's seeing our misery and acting to relieve it. He shows mercy when he sees his people suffering in Egypt and rescues them through Moses. At times God displays mercy by withholding deserved punishment. His mercy, seen in the Old Testament, overflows in the New Testament. This is especially true of Jesus, who has compassion for the weary and lost crowds. Mainly, God's mercy, which excludes human efforts to save oneself, brings salvation. His mercy moves his people to praise him and to show mercy to others (Ps 103:10; Matt 9:36; Eph 4:32; Titus 3:5). *See also* grace of God.

Messiah—God's anointed Deliverer of Israel and the nations, Jesus Christ. The words *Messiah* in Hebrew and *Christ* in Greek mean "anointed one." In the Old Testament, various people are "anointed ones," including Israel's kings (1 Sam 16:12–13), her priests (Exod 40:13, 15), and even Cyrus, king of Persia (Isa 45:1). Most important, the word and synonyms designate the promised King, the Messiah, who would deliver God's people—including Gentiles (42:1–7)—judge the wicked, and usher in God's kingdom (9:6–7). God speaks through Peter in identifying Jesus as "the Messiah, the Son of the living God" (Matt 16:16–17). The title "Christ" eventually becomes part of Jesus's name so that he is called "Jesus Christ" and "Christ Jesus." Jesus is truly anointed by the Spirit (3:16) and fulfills messianic prophecies (Acts 4:24–28). He performs messianic deeds (Matt 11:2–6) and pours out the Spirit on the church at Pentecost (Acts 2:1–21).

As a result, God exalts him to his right hand as "Lord and Christ" (v. 36 ESV). *See also* Christ's names and titles.

Messiah and the Spirit—*See* Holy Spirit's works.

metaphysics—the philosophical study that seeks to determine the ultimate nature of reality lying beyond the physical domain. The two branches of metaphysics are ontology, the study of being, and cosmology, the study of the origin of the universe. Metaphysics is one of the four main branches of philosophy. *See also* epistemology; ethics; logic.

Methodists—Protestant Christians inspired by the teachings of John Wesley. In the eighteenth century, John, his brother Charles, and friend George Whitefield sought to reform the Church of England. They did not intend to split from the Church, but a separation gradually occurred as congregations were planted and Wesley's theology developed. Doctrinal beliefs of Methodists include free will, inward assurance of salvation from the Spirit, and the pursuit of perfection. Under Wesley's leadership, Methodists became leaders in social issues, including prison reform and the abolition of slavery. Charles Wesley wrote thousands of hymns and stirred a rich musical tradition. Although the Methodist churches in America and Great Britain are declining, there is rapid growth in Korea. *See* Wesley, John; Wesley, Susanna; Wesleyanism.

midtribulationism—*See* rapture.

millennium—the thousand years of Rev 20:1–6. Evangelicals hold four views regarding this period: amillennialism, postmillennialism, historic premillennialism, and dispensational premillennialism. Amillennialism holds that the millennium describes the souls of dead believers reigning now with Jesus in heaven. The millennium, then, is present and describes the intermediate state. Christ will reign on earth forever in the future eternal state. The binding of Satan means he cannot prevent the spread of the gospel during the present age. Amillennialists hold that Christ will return *after* the millennium. The Second Coming will be a single event, at which he will bless his people and judge the lost. There will be one general resurrection of the dead, involving both the righteous and unrighteous.

Postmillennialism holds that the current age gradually merges into the millennium because a majority of the world will believe the gospel. Postmillennialists agree with all Christians that Christ will reign on the new earth forever. The binding of Satan means that the evil one cannot prevent the spread of the gospel now. As the name *post*millennialism implies, Christ will return *after* the millennium. Like amillennialists, post-millennialists hold that Christ's return is a single event and that there will be one general resurrection of all people. Historic premillennialism holds that the millennium is Christ's reign on earth for a thousand years after his return and before the eternal state. Premillennialism rejects the post-millennial view that the world will be gradually Christianized as a majority of people believe the gospel. Instead, Christ's coming will usher in the millennium powerfully and immediately. The binding of Satan means he will be unable to deceive the nations during the future millennium. His exten-sive binding does not describe the current rebellious age but partially accounts for the righteousness and peace of Christ's universal millennial reign. As its name implies, *pre*millennialism maintains that Christ will come back *before* the thousand years. Historic premillennialism agrees with the previous two views that the Second Coming will be a single event. Unlike those views, historic premillennialism holds to two resurrections, one before and one after the millennium. Deceased saints will be raised before the millennium to participate in it. After the millennium, other believers who died during the thousand years will be raised along with all the wicked. Dispensational premillennialism agrees with historic pre-millennialists that the millennium refers to Christ's thousand-year reign on earth after his return and before the new earth. Traditionally, dispen-sationalists have taught a Jewish character to the millennium, including a restored temple and blood sacrifices. Dispensational premillennialists agree with historic premillennialists that the binding of Satan means he will be unable to deceive the nations during the future millennium and that Christ's return will occur *before* the millennium. Unique to dispensa-tional premillennialism is the view that the Second Coming will occur in two stages: the mid-air rapture of the church before the tribulation and the Second Coming to earth after the tribulation and before the millennium. Historic premillennialism holds to two future resurrections, one before and one after the millennium. Dispensational premillennialism adds a third resurrection: Church saints, including resurrected ones, will be raptured to heaven before the great tribulation on earth. Jewish believers will be raised from the dead to participate in the Jewish millennium on earth. People who have come to Christ during the millennium, along with all the wicked, will be raised after the millennium to appear before God at the Last Judgment. Although contradictory understandings of Revelation 20 cannot be correct, we need not so emphasize the differences between the millennial views that we miss their common core beliefs. Christians from the first to the twenty-first century have held four eschatological truths in common: Christ's return, the resurrection of the dead, the Last Judgment, and eternal heaven and hell. *See also* heaven; hell; Last Judgment; new heavens and new earth; resurrection; Second Coming; tribulation.

mission—the goal and task of the church to carry the gospel to the world based on Jesus's command to disciple the nations. God is a missional God, for he seeks out his fallen image bearers and makes the first promise of the gospel to them (Gen 3:15). He chooses Israel out of all the peoples on earth, liberates them from Egyptian bondage, and tasks them to be his "kingdom of priests and . . . holy nation" before the world (Exod 19:6). Although Israel largely fails to fulfill this task, God promises to send a Messiah, who would deliver Israel and be a light to the nations (Isa 49:6). Jesus is that Messiah (Christ), and, based on Jesus's life, death, resurrection, and pouring out of the Spirit, God begins the global mission of his church. In fulfillment of God's plan, he commissions his Son to be the Savior of the world and commissions his church to take the good news to the ends of the earth (Matt 28:18–20). *See also* Carmichael, Amy; church, marks; Eareckson Tada, Joni; gospel; Great Commission; Padilla, René.

modalism—*See* Trinity.

Modalistic Monarchianism—*See* Trinity.

modernism—an intellectual and cultural worldview ranging from the eighteenth-century Enlightenment to early twenty-first-century postmodernism. Modernism had great confidence that universal reason and science would provide an objective foundation for knowledge, and that such

knowledge leads to human autonomy and unlimited progress in governmental and scientific achievements. *See also* ecumenism; evangelicalism;
liberalism; neoorthodoxy; postmodernism.

Moltmann, Jürgen (1926–)—a famous twentieth-century theologian.
Pervading all his work is the theme of hope, introduced in his *Theology of
Hope* (1964), whereby he interprets the present, even the present life of
God, in light of Christ's future return to give hope to the oppressed. In *The
Crucified God* (1972), he argues that God's love necessitates his suffering
in the cross of Christ, thereby identifying with the world's suffering. In
so doing, Moltmann rejects the church's historic position that God does
not suffer and raises question about substitutionary atonement. In *The
Trinity and the Kingdom*, Moltmann rejects the traditional doctrine of the
Trinity for social trinitarianism, which stresses the relationships between
the three divine persons, so as to question God's unity. He also rejects
God's lordship and authority, and denies any order among the trinitarian
persons. He endorses panentheism, holding to a necessary and recipro-
cal relation between God and the world; it drives Moltmann's promotion
of liberation theology, ecology, and feminism. *See also* anthropopathism;
Christ's saving work; Christ's saving work, biblical images; immutability
of God; moral influence theory; panentheism; Second Coming; Trinity.

monergism/synergism—two views that attempt to answer the question,
Who brings about salvation? Monergism says that it is God alone, while
synergism says that God and humans work together to bring about salvation. Synergism credits God with initiating salvation, to which humans
must respond positively and cooperate with God's grace to be saved. By
contrast, monergism holds that God alone initiates and completes salvation. By God's grace, humans believe the gospel and are saved. *See also*
Arminianism; Calvinism; free will; sovereignty of God.

monism—the philosophical view that reality is composed of one substance or principle. It opposes dualism which holds that reality is composed of two substances or principles. Both materialism and idealism are
monistic. Materialism holds that all reality is matter while idealism holds

that all reality is spirit. *See also* creation; dualism; eternity of God; humanity, makeup; idealism; intermediate state; materialism; naturalism.

Monophysitism—*See* Christ's unity.

moral influence theory—*See* Christ's saving work, historical views.

Mosaic covenant—*See* covenant(s); new covenant.

Mosaic law—*See* law; law, uses; Ten Commandments.

mutual indwelling—*See* Trinity.

mystical union—*See* union with Christ.

mysticism—religious practice seeking direct personal knowledge of God rather than intellectual knowledge of him. Mysticism strives for experience of the divine that ordinarily bypasses the traditional means of grace. For this reason, most believers rightly distrust mysticism. Mystics seek to reach God through intuition and contemplation. Other religions, including Buddhism and Kabbalah (secret Jewish mysticism), practice mysticism. Famous Christian mystics include Bernard of Clairvaux (twelfth century), Meister Eckhart (fourteenth century), and Teresa of Ávila (seventeenth century). *See also* apophatic theology; means of grace; prayer; spiritual disciplines; Teresa of Ávila.

Nn

natural headship—*See* sin.

natural revelation—*See* revelation.

natural theology—a type of philosophy that argues for the existence and attributes of God based on reason, studying general revelation without reference to special revelation in Scripture. Thomas Aquinas argued that humans can attain some truths about God this way, but not others, such as the Trinity, for which scriptural revelation is required. Karl Barth combated natural theology, while Emil Brunner defended it. Recently, intelligent design theory has appealed to natural theology, while the New Atheism movement has opposed it. *See also* Aquinas, Thomas; existence of God, arguments for the; revelation.

naturalism—the philosophical view that everything comes from natural causes, thus excluding supernaturalism. Naturalism, also known as materialism, is atheistic. *See also* agnosticism; apatheism; atheism; dualism; idealism; materialism; monism.

naturalistic evolution—*See* humanity, origin.

necessity of Scripture—*See* Scripture; Scripture, attributes.

neoorthodox view of inspiration—*See* inspiration; inspiration, views.

neoorthodoxy—influential twentieth-century Protestant theological movement in Europe and America, led by Karl Barth, Emil Brunner, and Reinhold Niebuhr. The movement is called "neoorthodox" because they spoke the traditional language of the Bible and orthodox theology rather than that of the theological liberalism of their training. They disliked the term *neoorthodoxy*, however, because they accepted modern critical methods of studying the Bible and held that parts of the Bible are not true. The Word is Jesus Christ become man for our salvation. North American neoorthodox theologians like Niebuhr sought to understand controversial social issues from a Christian viewpoint. Neoorthodoxy declined in the 1970s, when liberation theologies were ascending. Evangelicals critiqued neoorthodoxy for rejecting an orthodox view of Scripture, denying a historical fall, and inclining toward universalism. *See also* Barth, Karl; ecumenism; evangelicalism; liberalism; modernism; poor, the; truth; universalism.

Nestorianism—*See* Christ's unity; Council of Chalcedon.

new covenant—the culmination of the Bible's covenants, featuring the full forgiveness of sins because of the death of Jesus, its Mediator. The Old Testament prophets often look forward to a great future work of God. Jeremiah 31:31–34, which uses the term "new covenant," is most famous because Hebrews quotes it (Heb 8:8–12; 10:16–17). The new covenant replaces the Mosaic covenant, which disobedient Israel failed to keep. In its place, God promises to make a new covenant, which would repeat the familiar refrain "I will be their God, and they will be my people" (Ezek 37:27; see also Jer 24:7), showing continuity with the covenants that went before, especially the Abrahamic covenant. In it, God enters into covenant with Abraham and his descendants, promising to be their God, making them into a great nation, and giving them the Promised Land. Paul explains that the Abrahamic covenant is the basis for the new covenant in Christ (Gal 3:16–18). What is new about the new covenant? It is not the internalization of the law with responsive hearts, for this idea appears in the law (Deut 6:4–6; 11:18). Rather, mercifully considering Israel's inability to keep the covenant, God promises universal knowledge of himself and total forgiveness: "They will all know me, from the least to the greatest. . . . For I will forgive their iniquity and never again remember their sin" (Jer 31:34). The new covenant is new because it depends not on human faithfulness but on divine faithfulness. Five times in Jeremiah 31 God says "I will," indicating that he will sovereignly enact this covenant. Hebrews 8:6–13 indicates that Jesus fulfills the new covenant. Indeed, at the Last Supper, Jesus says, "This cup is the new covenant in my blood, which is poured out for you" (Luke 22:20). Because Jesus, the Mediator of the new covenant (Heb 9:15; 12:24), inaugurates the covenant with his blood and obtains eternal redemption, believers have "the promise of the eternal inheritance" (9:15). The restoration of the Jews to the Promised Land after the exile is the beginning of the fulfillment of new covenant promises. But this is only a beginning, for its ultimate consummation is in the new heavens and new earth. Only then will there be full and universal knowledge of God and full enjoyment of the forgiveness of sins. *See also* covenant(s).

new heavens and new earth—the future cleansed and renewed world and final state of the redeemed. The culmination of future hope is that "the creation itself will . . . be set free from the bondage to decay into the glorious freedom of God's children" (Rom 8:21). The redemption of God's world and people will occur together (vv. 22–23). The consummation of God's plan of salvation is not a disembodied existence in heaven but a resurrected holistic one on the new earth. This will happen after Jesus returns, the dead are raised, and the Last Judgment occurs. Only then will there be complete knowledge of God and full enjoyment of the forgiveness of sins. Believers will inherit God and the new heavens and new earth (1 Cor 3:21–23; Rev 21:3). *See also* heaven; hell; humanity, states; preterism; resurrection.

new humanity—*See* church, pictures.

new Jerusalem—*See* heaven; new heavens and new earth.

Nicene Creed (325)—a Christian statement of faith, originated from the first ecumenical council of the church (at Nicaea), affirming the deity of Christ against Arianism. Arius, a clergyman of Alexandria, denied the deity of Christ and triggered the Arian controversy. Bishop Alexander, Athanasius, and their allies wrote the creed to clarify major beliefs of the Christian faith in response to the popularity of Arius's views. The creed teaches that the Son shares the essence of deity with the Father. In rejection of Arianism, which held that the Son is God's first creature, the creed asserts that the Son is not a created being but is fully divine. *See also* Apostles' Creed; Athanasius; Christ's deity; Christ's deity, denials; Council of Nicaea; *homoousios*.

Noahic covenant—*See* covenant(s).

nominalism—*See* realism and nominalism.

Oo

obedience—doing what God has commanded his people to do. One of Scripture's characteristics is that, because God is its origin, it shares his authority. God alone has the right to impart truth and command our obedience. We do not stand over the Word of God, judging it. Rather, it is over us, and our responsibility is to believe and humbly obey it. Jesus spoke plainly: "If you love me, you will keep my commands" (John 14:15). Jesus set a high example of obedience as the God-man, always submissive to the Father (15:10). *See also* conscience; Scripture, attributes; virtues, Christian; will of God.

offices of the church—*See* church, government.

old covenant—*See* covenant(s).

old earth creationism—*See* humanity, origin.

omnipotence of God—the almighty God's unlimited power to do anything he chooses to do. His being all-powerful means he can do anything that power can do. God's power is linked to all his perfections, including love, holiness, and goodness (Ps 147:5; Isa 40:26; Matt 19:26; Eph 1:18–19). *See also* attributes of God; problem of evil; sovereignty of God.

omnipresence of God—God's attribute as a spirit of being wholly present everywhere at once. He is transcendent over (above and beyond) his creation: "God is enthroned above the circle of the earth" (Isa 40:22), so that "even heaven, the highest heaven, cannot contain" him (1 Kgs 8:27). He is also immanent (present) in his creation, though not a part of it: "in him we live and move and have our being" (Acts 17:28). Scripture speaks of God as both transcendent and immanent at once (Jer 23:23–24). Though omnipresent, God manifests his presence in a special way at specific times and places, as in the Old Testament tabernacle and temple (Exod 40:34–35; 1 Kgs 8:10–11). God is especially present with his people: "he gathers the lambs in his arms" (Isa 40:11; cf. Ps 139:7–9). In the New Testament, God becomes incarnate in Jesus (John 1:14), and God manifests his special presence now indwelling believers, individually (1 Cor 6:19) and corporately (3:16). He will be especially present with his people forever on the new earth (Rev 21:3). *See also* attributes of God.

omniscience of God—God's attribute of being unlimited in knowledge. Because his understanding is infinite, he knows the past, present, and future. There are hidden things that belong to God alone, yet he reveals some of them so that we may know and obey him (Deut 29:29; Ps 147:5; Rom 11:33–34; Heb 4:13). *See also* attributes of God; foreknowledge; wisdom of God.

ontological Trinity—*See* Trinity, ontological/economic.

ontology—the philosophical study of being. It is distinguished from epistemology, which deals with the study of knowing. Much of the history of philosophy treats ontological disputes between those affirming or denying whether particular categories—nonphysical minds, a world existing outside the mind, free will, and God—exist. After it was rejected by logical positivism's rejection of metaphysics, ontology was revived in the mid-twentieth century by the American philosopher W. V. O. Quine. It is a subset of metaphysics, the philosophical study of the real nature of things. *See also* epistemology; ethics; logic; metaphysics.

open theism—the view that God neither controls nor knows the future; also called openness theology, the open view of God, or free will theism. Open theists believe that God's primary attribute is love, and that in love he gives humans the freedom to choose or reject him. They also assert that humans have libertarian free will and, since God and humans are free, his knowledge is dynamic and his providence flexible. Though all-powerful, he limits his control so we can freely cooperate with him in salvation. Though God is all-knowing, his knowledge excludes the future, for the future is "open" and unknowable, even to God. Open theism is a serious error, for, according to Scripture, God controls (Ps 33:10–11; 135:6; 139:16; Dan 4:34–35) and knows (Isa 42:8–9; 44:6–7; 46:9–10) the future. Ultimately, open theism reduces God's greatness, sovereignty, and glory and undermines Christians' confidence that they can trust God concerning the future. *See also* compatibilism; free will; incompatibilism; love of God; omnipotence of God; omniscience of God; providence.

ordinances or sacraments—sacred rites that God gives to his people to celebrate. *Ordinance* refers to the fact that God has ordained them. *Sacrament* means "holy sign." These include circumcision and Passover in the Old Testament and baptism and the Lord's Supper in the New. Roman Catholicism has seven sacraments: baptism, Eucharist, confirmation, penance and reconciliation, extreme unction (anointing the sick), matrimony, and holy orders (ordination). Contrary to these claims, Jesus gave only two ordinances to his church: baptism and the Lord's Supper. Through the Word and ordinances, God ministers to our five senses. The Word addresses our ears and eyes, and God reinforces the spoken and written Word with touch, taste, and smell of the ordinances. Jesus wanted the church always to remember the gospel, so he commanded that it be preached (Matt 28:19–20; cf. 2 Tim 2:2), and he instituted baptism (Matt 28:19) and the Lord's Supper (26:26–29) to dramatize the gospel. God preaches the gospel to us in baptism (Acts 2:38) and the Lord's Supper (1 Cor 11:26). *See also* baptism, views; church, marks; Lord's Supper; Roman Catholicism.

ordination—the solemn setting apart of someone to a church office or ministry.

Origen (185–253)—the most prolific scholar of the early church; nevertheless, he was condemned for heresy. Learned in Neoplatonist philosophy, he wrote *Against Celsus* to defend the faith against a Greek philosopher opposing Christianity. His massive *Hexapla* arranged six versions of the Old Testament in parallel columns. His biblical commentaries promoted allegorical interpretation. He is best known for *On First Principles*, a systematic presentation of the faith suffused with Christian Neoplatonism.

His Christology appears to be subordinationist, and he was condemned for universalism. *See also* universalism.

original sin—the effects of Adam's sin on his posterity that results in their being born sinful and alienated from God. *See* sin.

Owen, John (1616–1683)—English Nonconformist church leader, theologian, and academic administrator, who earned great respect for his character and keen intellect. He was a great preacher, and his abundant writings include *Doctrine of the Saints' Perseverance* (1654); *On the Mortification of Sin in Believers* (1656); *Of Temptation* (1658); a massive commentary on the Epistle to the Hebrews; a probing book on *Indwelling Sin*; *On the Holy Spirit* (1677–1678); and *The Doctrine of Justification* (1677). *See also* perseverance; preaching; temptation.

Pp

Padilla, René (1932–)—Ecuadorian evangelical missiologist known for creating the term *integral mission*. Serving in Latin America with the International Fellowship of Evangelical Students, he met university students bombarded with Marxism and ideas of revolution. From this environment arose liberation theology and Padilla's promotion of integral mission—Christianity's obligation both to preach the gospel and engage in social activism. At the Lausanne Conference (1974) his ideas went global and influenced evangelical mission strategy. His best-known book is *Mission between the Times: Essays on the Kingdom of God* (1985). *See also* Gutiérrez, Gustavo; liberation theology; mission.

panentheism—the view that God is in everything that exists. It understands God as affected by every event in the universe and thus growing in knowledge. Although panentheism sees a distinction between God and the world, it also sees both God and the world as a necessary whole. It differs from pantheism, which says God is all, and all is God. It also differs from biblical Christianity, which says God created all and cares for and directs his creation while maintaining a distinction between the Creator and his creatures. *See also* attributes of God; creation; incommunicable attributes of God; pantheism; providence.

Pannenberg, Wolfhart (1928–2014)—a prominent twentieth-century Lutheran theologian who pursued a rational theology based in history rather than in the human self, as his forebears did. He insists that theology must be public and open to discussion. He mastered secular disciplines, such as the philosophy of history, anthropology, and science to defend Christian truth claims. Pannenberg was an ecumenical theologian who emphasized the Trinity and later the church. In critique, his emphasis on reason reduces the Spirit's role in faith. He rejects the historic doctrines of Christ at Chalcedon but defends the historicity of Jesus's resurrection. However, since he holds that truth is future-oriented, and this colors all his work, we can only know Jesus's resurrection indirectly now; we will know it directly only when Jesus returns. His writings include *Jesus: God and Man*, and most important, a three-volume *Systematic Theology*. *See also* eschatology; Second Coming; Trinity.

pantheism—the view that God is everything, and everything is God. Pantheism thus erroneously confuses God with his world. The doctrine of creation refutes pantheism, for God alone existed before he made the world, and when he made it, it was and continues to be distinct from him. *See also* attributes of God; creation; eternity of God; omnipresence of God; panentheism; providence.

Paraclete—a transliteration into English of a Greek word used five times in the New Testament. John's Gospel uses it four times (14:16, 26; 15:26; 16:7) to refer to the Holy Spirit, where it is translated "Counselor" (a.k.a. 'Helper,' ESV; 'Comforter,' KJV; or 'Advocate,' NIV). In 1 John 2:1, the word refers to Jesus as our "advocate with the Father." *See also* Holy Spirit's names and descriptions.

paradise—*See* heaven.

parousia—*See* Second Coming.

passibility—*See* impassibility of God.

passive obedience of Christ—*See* Christ's obedience.

pastors—*See* church, government.

patience—*See* virtues, Christian.

patience of God—God's slowness to anger and his willingness to not always punish sin right away. God showed great patience with wicked people when he waited for Noah to build the ark and when he sent prophets to his people, who did not listen. God's patience relates to salvation, for he patiently endures rejecters of the gospel while he rescues believers. He wants us to be patient as we await Christ's return (Exod 34:6–7; Neh 9:30; Jas 1:19; 2 Pet 3:15). *See also* attributes of God; Second Coming.

peace—*See* virtues, Christian.

peccability—*See* impeccability.

pedobaptism—*See* infant baptism.

Pelagianism—*See* sin.

penal substitution—*See* Christ's saving work, biblical images; Christ's saving work, historical views; substitution.

penance—*See* ordinances or sacraments.

Pentecost—*See* Christ's saving work; kingdom of God.

Pentecostalism—a renewal movement beginning in the early twentieth century that teaches "second blessing" theology. Pentecostals hold to a high view of Scripture and salvation through faith in Christ, whom they believe will come again. They teach that the baptism of the Holy Spirit is a second work of grace and empowerment after conversion, of which speaking in tongues is evidence. They emphasize sign gifts, such as miracles, healing, prophecy, and tongues, and are leaders in worldwide missions and church planting. Pentecostalism is one of the fastest-growing and largest forms of Christianity. *See also* baptism of the Holy Spirit; charismatic gifts; Holy Spirit's filling; Holy Spirit's gifts; Holy Spirit's ministries; speaking in tongues.

people of God—*See* church, pictures.

perfectionism—the view that it is possible for believers to be freed from sin in this life. Associated especially with John Wesley, who taught that Christian perfection was not sinlessness but freedom from willful violation of a known law of God, it involves loving God so completely that love controls all thoughts, words, and deeds. Proponents interpret New Testament texts as teaching that it is possible for believers to attain a state in which they no longer sin but nonetheless must grow in grace (1 John 3:6, 9; 5:18). *See also* sanctification; sin; Wesley, John.

perichoresis—*See* Trinity.

persecution—the world's hostility toward and ill treatment of God's people. Believers in both Testaments are persecuted for their faith (Ps 119:84–88; Acts 8:1). Persecution takes various forms, including words (Matt 5:11) and violence (Acts 9:1–2). It is to be expected, for Jesus warned, "If they persecuted me, they will also persecute you" (John 15:20). And Paul said, "All who want to live a godly life in Christ Jesus will be persecuted" (2 Tim 3:12). Jesus blessed those persecuted because of him (Matt 5:11) and urged prayer for persecutors (v. 44). Persecution separates true from false Christians (13:21). Because of union between Christ and his own, persecuting them is persecuting him (Acts 9:4). Christians suffer but know that not even persecution can separate them from God's love in Christ (Rom 8:35–39). The returning Christ will bring relief to persecuted believers and judge their enemies with eternal separation from God (2 Thess 1:5–10). *See also* prayer; sanctification; union with Christ.

perseverance—a doctrine that encompasses both God's keeping his saints saved (preservation) and also their continuing to live for him. God graciously saves and keeps his own. Jesus gives his sheep eternal life and says that they will never perish, for they are safe in his and the Father's hands (John 10:28–30). Paul likewise affirms God's preservation: "There is now no condemnation for those in Christ Jesus" (Rom 8:1). He advances arguments for preservation from God's plan, sovereignty, justice, and love (vv. 29–39). Hebrews says that Christ "is able to save completely" his people (7:24–25). Peter too affirms preservation (1 Pet 1:3–5). Scripture teaches that true believers must and will continue in the faith. Our perseverance in faith, love, and holiness highlights the reality of our profession. True believers persevere in faith (John 6:66–69; Col 1:22–23; Heb 10:36). We may waver but will never completely and totally reject the gospel. True believers also persevere in love. When God gives new life, he gives a new heart that loves him and others. Our love for God and others is never perfect in this life, but it is real. A lack of love reveals a lack of salvation, and persevering love strengthens assurance (1 John 3:10, 13–15). Finally, true believers persevere in holiness. God saves us not based on our holiness but to holiness (Eph 2:8–10; Titus 3:4–8). Consistently failing to live for God is a bad sign, for everyone God saves pursues holiness (Heb 12:14). *See also* application of salvation; assurance of salvation; preservation; providence.

person of Christ—*See* Christ's person and work.

personality of God—God's being as a divine person, not an impersonal force. Human beings are persons because he has made us in his image. God has the qualities of personality, including intelligence, self-awareness, and the ability to relate to others. He has intelligence, for he is all-knowing. God has self-awareness, for he has a name and invites us to pray to him. He relates to others, for he loves his people deeply (Exod 3:14; Col 4:2; 1 John 3:20; 4:9–11). *See also* attributes of God; image of God (*imago Dei*); omniscience of God; prayer.

personality of the Spirit—*See* Holy Spirit's personality.

perspicuity of Scripture—*See* Scripture; Scripture, attributes.

philosophical theology—a branch of philosophy that uses philosophical methods to analyze and understand theological truths. Philosophical theology began in the eighteenth century when theologians sought to defend biblical revelation against philosophical attacks. Contemporary philosophers who argue from a Christian framework include William Lane Craig and James K. A. Smith. *See also* apologetics; empiricism; natural theology; rationalism.

Pietism—a late seventeenth-century Lutheran movement, urging that Christianity is not only a system of orthodox theology but a guide for Christian living. Pastor Philipp Spener's *Pious Desires* promoted Bible study, prayer, and personal godliness. Pietism impacted worldwide Christianity. *See also* sanctification; spiritual disciplines; spirituality.

Platonism—the philosophy of Plato (c. 428–347 BC), a Greek philosopher who taught Aristotle and shaped Western thought and Christian theology.

Paramount in his thought was a distinction between two worlds, the world in which we live and a world of transcendent and eternal realities, which Plato called forms. In this view, our changing world is filled with creatures that are imperfect copies of the absolute, eternal forms. The highest form is the Good. When we seek to know our world through our senses, we err and need philosophical guidance. The body hinders the soul in its contemplation of truth, but death frees the soul from the body, and the soul contemplates truth directly. Platonism's influence on Christianity includes God as a spiritual being and the Good, the division between a physical body and a spiritual soul, the soul's immortality, and heaven as a perfect world. He wrote his famous Dialogues and *The Republic*. *See also* Aristotelianism; heaven; humanity, makeup; spirituality of God.

plenary inspiration—*See* inspiration; inspiration, views.

pluralism—*See* exclusivism/inclusivism/pluralism.

pneumatology—in Christian theology, the study of the doctrine of the Holy Spirit, including his personality, deity, works, and ministries.

poor, the—the deprived and needy, on whom God has compassion. He cares for the poor (Deut 15:7–11; Ps 72:12), whom his people should protect (Deut 10:19; Amos 5:11–12). Jesus condemned the oppressive rich and defended the oppressed poor (Matt 25:34–46). James teaches that believers must show concern for the poor (1:27), reflecting the first-century church's attitude (Gal 2:9–10). God chose poor people for salvation (Jas 2:5), so God's people should not discriminate against them (2:1–13). John is bold: "If anyone has this world's goods and sees a fellow believer in need but withholds compassion from him—how does God's love reside in him?" (1 John 3:17). *See also* love of God.

pope—*See* church, government; Roman Catholicism.

postmillennialism—*See* millennium.

postmodernism—intellectual and cultural developments of the late twentieth and early twenty-first centuries marked by a rejection of modernism and its emphasis on reason. Postmodernism denies that there is universal, objective knowledge, and thus regards all truth claims as culturally relative. Universal reason and objective science are viewed as impossible since individuals and communities construct reality. Evangelicals reject modernism's claim of the all-competence of reason but also fault postmodernism for its rejection of truth and the authority of God's Word. Scripture teaches the existence, transcendence, and truthfulness of God and the resultant fact that his Word is true because it corresponds to reality (Ps 119:160; John 17:17; 2 Tim 2:15). *See also* exclusivism/inclusivism/pluralism; modernism; relativism; truth; truthfulness of God.

postmortem evangelism—the view that God gives people a chance after death to respond to the gospel and be saved. Proponents appeal to 1 Peter (3:18–20; 4:6). Some hold that only the unevangelized in this life have a postmortem opportunity. Others hold that those who rejected Christ in this life get another opportunity after death. Postmortem evangelism is a serious error because destinies are fixed by people's response to Jesus in this life (John 3:17–18), death marks the end of opportunity to believe (John 8:21, 24), and judgment follows death (Heb 9:27). *See also* gospel; Great Commission; heaven; hell; mission.

posttribulationism—*See* rapture.

pouring, baptism by—*See* baptism, mode.

practical theology—the study of ways theology is applied to individuals and the church. God uses theology to improve what we believe and how we live. Theology summons us to proper ways of thinking, believing, loving, and obeying, all for ourselves and the church. *See also* doctrine; systematic theology; theological method.

praise—*See* worship.

prayer—speaking to God in faith. Biblically, prayer takes various forms: adoration of God, thanksgiving for blessings, confession of sin, intercession for others, and petition for ourselves. Although it is not necessary to always use it, a complete pattern for prayer is to pray to God the Father, through the Son, in the Spirit. Prayer is usually addressed to the Father as the First Person of the Trinity, following Jesus's example (John 17:1).

Prayer is made through the Son, the Mediator between God and human beings, with the confidence born of trust in his death and resurrection (16:23–24). Prayer is offered in the power of the Spirit (Eph 6:18), who himself makes intercession for us according to God's will (Rom 8:26–27). Believers must pray to God in faith (Jas 1:6–8), submitting to his will (1 John 5:14–15). *See also* confession (1); Holy Spirit's ministries; Lord's Prayer; mediator.

preaching—proclaiming the Word of God, especially the gospel. Preaching is proclaiming the gospel according to biblical teaching, in the power of the Holy Spirit. This teaching includes the facts that salvation is by God's grace alone through faith alone in Christ alone (Eph 2:8–9). It presents Jesus as the world's only Savior (John 14:6; Acts 4:12) and his death and resurrection as the only way of salvation from sin and hell (1 Cor 15:3–4). Although all believers are to share their faith (1 Thess 1:8), God gives his church pastors and teachers (Eph 4:11), whose responsibilities include preaching the Word (2 Tim 4:2). Homiletics is that branch of practical theology that treats the preparation and practice of sermons. *See also* church, government; church, marks; gospel.

predestination—*See* election.

prediction/fulfillment—*See* prophecy; salvation history.

preexistence of Christ—the Son of God's existence before his incarnation. The Bible teaches this through appearances of the Son in the Old Testament (Isa 6:5; John 12:41), John's teaching (John 1:1–3, 15), and affirmations of Paul (Phil 2:6; Col 1:16–17). *See also* Christ's incarnation; deity of Christ.

Presbyterian church government—*See* church, government.

Presbyterians—Protestant Christians who belong to the Reformed tradition, stemming from John Calvin and later from Great Britain, especially Scotland. The name comes from their form of church government, for local churches are led by presbyters (elders). Churches belong to presbyteries, which govern a geographical area, and the largest governing body is the general assembly. Presbyterians hold to biblical authority, God's sovereignty, and salvation by grace through faith. They practice infant baptism and are committed to evangelism, church planting, and missions. Evangelical Presbyterians uphold the Westminster Confession of Faith and the Larger and Shorter Catechisms as formulations of faith subordinate to Scripture. *See also* Calvin, John; church, government; Reformation.

presence of God—*See* heaven.

present age—*See* two ages.

preservation—(1) the aspect of God's providence whereby he maintains his creation; (2) the work of God whereby he keeps believers saved to the end so they do not fall away from salvation. *See also* assurance of salvation; perseverance; providence.

preterism—the erroneous view that most (partial preterism) or all (full preterism) of the last things predicted in Scripture, especially in Revelation, have already taken place, including Christ's return, the resurrection, the Last Judgment, heaven, and hell. On the contrary, believers throughout church history have rightly regarded these five truths as the most important *future* events. *See also* heaven; hell; Last Judgment; resurrection; Second Coming.

pretribulationism—*See* rapture.

prevenient grace—grace that comes before and leads to salvation. John Wesley and Wesleyanism teach that, although since the fall people are born sinners, God's preceding grace nullifies the effects of original sin on the will, enabling all to believe and be saved if they exercise this gracious ability. Wesleyanism thus teaches that prevenient grace is universal and can be accepted or rejected. Augustine, Calvin, and Calvinism teach that prevenient grace is particular and efficacious, overcoming the bondage of the will and enabling all those chosen by God to believe and be saved. *See also* Arminianism; Arminius, James; compatibilism; free will; grace of God; incompatibilism; sin; Wesley, John.

priesthood of believers—the belief of Protestants since the Reformation that, because of Christ the Mediator, all believers have direct access to

God without human intermediaries and are able to serve him. The priesthood of believers stands in opposition to the Roman Catholic and Eastern Orthodox sacrament of Holy Orders, which teaches that by virtue of ordination by a bishop, priests receive special power to serve God. First Peter 2:9 teaches the priesthood of believers: "But you are a chosen race, a royal priesthood . . . so that you may proclaim the praises of the one who called you out of darkness into his marvelous light." *See also* Eastern Orthodoxy; mediator; Reformation; Roman Catholicism.

problem of evil—the challenge of how to reconcile the existence of evil, God's omnipotence, and God's goodness. The existence of evil calls into question either God's power or goodness. If he has power to stop evil and does not, it seems to challenge his goodness. If he is good and does not stop evil, it seems to challenge his power. An attempt to solve the problem of evil is called a theodicy. *See also* goodness of God; omnipotence of God; suffering; theodicy.

process theology—twentieth-century theological movement begun by Alfred North Whitehead that views God as "bipolar." It holds that reality is evolving, and God relates so strongly to it that he too is in process and developing. God has two poles: a "primordial" pole, in which he is transcendent, timeless, and good; and a "consequent" pole, by which he is immanent, temporal, mutable, and an essential part of the changing process of the world. Process theology holds that God is not omnipotent but persuasive. Proponents include Charles Hartshorne, John B. Cobb Jr., and Marjorie Suchocki. Key criticisms are that process theology violates the Creator/creature distinction and makes God dependent on the world. *See also* creation; eternity of God; omnipotence of God; omniscience of God.

profession of faith—*See* confession (2).

progressive creationism—*See* humanity, origin.

progressive revelation—*See* revelation, progressive.

prolegomenon, prolegomena—in Christian theology, matters introductory to the study of doctrines, including the nature, task, sources, and method of theology.

prophecy—in Scripture, God's speaking through human beings, called prophets (2 Pet 1:20–21). God chose and called prophets to speak his Word to his people, to prophesy. God distinguishes true prophets from false ones (Deut 18:15–22). God's prophets speak first to their own time and sometimes make future predictions. God is able to predict future fulfillments because of his omniscience and providence. *See also* omniscience of God; providence; Scripture.

propitiation—the satisfaction of God's wrath, particularly through Christ's substitutionary death on the cross, which is the basis for God's declaring sinners righteous in Christ (justification) (Rom 3:25–26 ESV; 1 John 4:10 ESV). *See also* Christ's saving work, biblical images; Christ's saving work, historical views; justification; substitution; wrath of God.

proposition—a meaningful, rational statement whose truthfulness can be verified. Scripture contains propositions, and we use propositions to express theological truths. Propositionalism defends doctrines by stating them in propositions capable of logical demonstration. This helpfully reminds us of Scripture's rational character, but risks reducing all types of biblical literature to propositions. Scripture, however, also contains poetry, proverbs, parables, and other literary forms. Propositionalism can also miss elements of mystery, emotion, and practical outworking in thinking about God. *See also* epistemology; logic.

Protestantism—*See* Reformation.

protoevangelium (**"first gospel"**)—the first mention of God's promise of salvation. God sought out Adam and Eve after the fall and confronted them. Amid God's words of judgment, he promised deliverance. God cursed the serpent, Satan's instrument: "I will put hostility between you and the woman, and between your offspring and her offspring. He will strike your head, and you will strike his heel" (Gen 3:15). Satan will deal the woman's offspring, the Redeemer, a blow. But he will deal Satan a fatal blow, wounding his head. As God's plan unfolds, we learn that Eve's offspring is Jesus, the eternal Son of God, who became a genuine human. Satan inspired (John 13:2) and energized (v. 27) Judas to betray Jesus to death on the cross. However, God is stronger than the devil, and one purpose of the Son's taking on flesh and blood is so that he could die to destroy the devil and deliver God's people (Heb 2:14–15). *See also* Christ's saving work, biblical images; gospel.

providence—God's ongoing work of maintaining and guiding his creation. Includes both preservation and government. Preservation is God's work of maintaining his creation, whereas government is his work of directing his creation toward his goals. God's preservation especially pertains to his people, whom he saves and keeps (Psalm 23; 33:10–22; 104:10–30; Isa 40:22–26; Acts 4:23–31; Col 1:17; Heb 1:3). *See also* assurance of salvation; creation; perseverance; preservation.

psychosomatic unity—*See* humanity, makeup.

punishment, eternal—*See* hell.

purgatory—*See* hell; intermediate state.

Puritanism—a sixteenth- and seventeenth-century movement of English Protestants to purify the Church of England because the English Reformation had not gone far enough. Puritans sought greater simplicity of worship; they rejected Episcopal church government and Anglican ritual. They also emphasized biblical and theological truth, preaching, and spiritual earnestness. The Puritans held to Calvinist and covenant theology. They founded Congregationalist and Presbyterian churches in England and the New England colonies. Major Puritans were John Owen and Jonathan Edwards. *See also* Calvin, John; church, government; covenant theology; Reformation.

Rr

Radical Reformation—sixteenth-century groups who opposed both the Roman Catholic Church and Lutheran and Calvinist churches, all of which persecuted them for their views. Radicals included intellectuals who denied the Trinity and fanatics who took over cities as they heralded the end of the world. The most important groups were the Anabaptists, who held that Zwingli and Luther did not go far enough. In response Zwingli, Luther, and later Calvin rejected the Anabaptists as radical too and promoted their persecution. Notable Anabaptist leaders included Menno Simons and Jacob Hutter. In general, Anabaptists held to a rejection of infant baptism for the practice of adult baptism after repentance, the Lord's Supper as a memorial for the baptized, free will, churches free from state control, and opposition to secular laws and military service. Later, separatist forms of Anabaptism included Mennonites, Amish, and Hutterites. *See also* Calvin, John; Luther, Martin; Reformation; Zwingli, Ulrich.

Rahner, Karl (1904–1984)—the leading Roman Catholic theologian of the twentieth century. Influenced by Martin Heidegger, Rahner integrated existential philosophy with Thomas Aquinas's theology. His starting point was the idea that all humans as transcendent beings have knowledge of God that comes through their experience of searching for meaning. He is well known for identifying the Trinity in itself (immanent Trinity) with the Trinity revealed in history (economic Trinity). He was a philosophical theologian who endorsed "anonymous Christianity," the idea that people who do not confess Jesus may have a saving relationship with God. In 1962 Pope John XXIII appointed Rahner an expert advisor to Vatican II, which he significantly influenced. Among his writings are a systematic theology, *Foundations for Christian Faith*, and his best-known, twenty-three-volume, diverse collection of essays, *Theological Investigations*. *See also* Aquinas, Thomas; exclusivism/inclusivism/pluralism; Roman Catholicism; Trinity; Trinity, ontological/economic.

ransom—*See* Christ's saving work, biblical images; Christ's saving work, historical views.

ransom-to-Satan view—*See* Christ's saving work, historical views.

rapture—in premillennial eschatology, the event associated with the view that Christ will return in the air to take the church out of the world. Christ will come again to take up all living believers along with the bodies of resurrected deceased ones to join him in heaven. Premillennialists disagree as to whether the rapture will occur before (pretribulationism), during (midtribulationism), or after (posttribulationism) the tribulation. Advocates distinguish the rapture from Christ's second coming to earth after the millennium and appeal to 1 Thess 4:15–17 for support. *See also* millennium; Second Coming; tribulation.

rationalism—the philosophy holding that reason, not sensory experience, is the supreme means of gaining knowledge. Descartes and Spinoza were early rationalists, for whom the seventeenth-century Age of Reason was named. Rationalists maintain that reality has a logical makeup that the mind can understand. They reject revelation and intuition as sources of knowledge. *See also* empiricism; epistemology; modernism; mysticism; postmodernism; relativism; truth; truthfulness of God.

realism (original sin)—*See* original sin; sin.

realism and nominalism—Realism is the philosophical idea that universals exist and are not merely the product of our minds. Nominalism claims that only particulars exist and that our minds create universals. Both views distinguish between universals (general abstract concepts) and particulars (specific concrete realities). If we ask if the universals of beauty and God's love (to cite two examples) are real, realists would say yes and nominalists would say no. Realism says that the universals of beauty and God's love exist independently of our thought. But nominalism denies their independent existence and says that "beauty" and "God's love" are simply names we give to specific things that we find pleasing to the eyes or to specific acts of kindness, respectively. Famous realists include Plato and Aristotle. Well-known nominalists include medieval philosopher William of Occam and the contemporary philosopher W. V. O. Quine. *See also* epistemology; metaphysics; ontology.

reason—*See* theology, sources.

reconciliation—*See* Christ's saving work, biblical images; reconciliation with others.

reconciliation with others—believers' state of being at peace not only with God but also with one another as a result of Christ's work on the cross. God in Christ, the peacemaker, reconciles God to us and us to God (2 Cor 5:18–19). As a result, we are no longer alienated from him but have peace with God through Christ. Paul teaches that God's reconciliation of humans is the basis for reconciliation between Jews and Gentiles in Christ (Eph 2:14–19). *See also* Christ's saving work, biblical images; church, pictures.

redemption—*See* Christ's saving work, biblical images; Christ's saving work, historical views.

redemptive history—*See* salvation history.

Reformation—the sixteenth-century religious movement in the Western church led by Martin Luther and John Calvin. Originally, the Reformers sought to reform the medieval Roman Catholic Church, but their efforts led to the founding of Protestantism. Ignited by discontent with unbiblical Catholic practices, such as the sale of indulgences, the movement generated debate about key issues and led to doctrinal reform. Most important were the supreme authority of Scripture and justification by faith, not works. The Reformation had far-reaching political, economic, and social effects. It led to the creation of separate denominations, including Lutheran, Reformed, and Anglican churches. The Catholic Church responded with a Counter-Reformation, begun by the Council of Trent (1545), and a new order, the Jesuits (1540). *See also* Augsburg Confession;

Calvin, John; Erasmus; justification; Knox, John; Luther, Martin; Radical Reformation; Reformation *solas*; Scripture, attributes; Westminster Confession of Faith; Zwingli, Ulrich.

Reformation *solas*—five Latin phrases that summarize the Protestant Reformers' essential teaching about the Christian faith, especially salvation. (1) *Sola scriptura* ("Scripture alone"): the Bible alone is our supreme authority for faith and practice. (2) *Sola fide* ("faith alone"): we are saved through faith in Jesus Christ alone, not good works. (3) *Sola gratia* ("grace alone"): we are saved by God's grace alone. (4) *Solus Christus* ("Christ alone"): Jesus Christ alone is our Lord and Savior and the only Mediator between God and men. (5) *Soli Deo gloria* ("to the glory of God alone"): all glory belongs to God alone, and by his grace our chief end is his glory. *See also* exclusivism/inclusivism/pluralism; faith; glory of God; grace of God; Reformation; *sola scriptura*.

Reformed theology—*See* Calvinism.

Reformed view of baptism—*See* baptism, views.

Reformed view of Lord's Supper—*See* Lord's Supper, views.

regeneration—God's giving new life in Christ. Before rebirth, we were dead in sin and unable to revive ourselves (Eph 2:1). In grace God made us alive with Christ (vv. 4–5). He caused us to be born again. Regeneration is like circumcision of the heart (Rom 2:29). God revives his people within, replacing a hard heart with a responsive one (Ezek 36:26–27). The Trinity is involved in our new birth. God the Father's vast mercy is the source of regeneration. The Son's resurrection is the basis of our new life (1 Pet 1:3). The Spirit is the mysterious and sovereign agent of the new birth who quickens us (John 3:8). The Spirit uses the Word of God to give us new life (1 Pet 1:23). Regeneration produces fruit, for those born of God believe that Jesus is the Christ (1 John 5:1), obey God daily (2:29), and love other believers (4:7–12). *See also* application of salvation; Christ's saving work; Holy Spirit's ministries; mercy of God; Trinity.

reign of Christ—*See* kingdom of God; millennium; new heavens and new earth.

relational view of image—*See* image of God (*imago Dei*).

relativism—the theory that truth and ethics are not absolute but are always relative to some framework. It holds that there is no privileged standpoint from which to view reality. It considers meaning and truth as relative to each person, group, or culture. Relativism points to three conclusions. First, there are no metaphysical realities, such as God, the human self, space, or time. Second, objective, universal truth and meaning are unobtainable. Third, there are no moral absolutes, but ethical norms depend on those who hold them. Evangelicalism views relativism as a major error and rejects these three conclusions. First, Scripture teaches the existence of the living and true God, one of whose attributes is truthfulness. Second, because this God has chosen to reveal himself in his Word, we can have genuine yet partial knowledge of his absolute truth. His Word is true because it corresponds to reality (Ps 119:160; John 17:17; 2 Tim 2:15). Third, because God is holy and has revealed himself truly in his holy Word, there are moral absolutes of truth and error and right and wrong. *See also* exclusivism/inclusivism/pluralism; modernism; postmodernism; truth; truthfulness of God.

repentance—turning away from sin. We distinguish repentance and faith, for they differ in direction. Repentance is directed toward sin and rejects it. Faith is directed toward God and believes in Christ. Sometimes both repentance and faith are listed together as conditions of salvation (Acts 20:21; Heb 6:1), but more frequently faith or repentance is mentioned solely (Matt 4:17; 2 Cor 7:10). Repentance and faith are distinguishable but inseparable. They are not two isolated conditions but the two aspects of conversion. Conversion is turning from sin (repentance) and turning to Christ (faith). When Scripture names only repentance or faith as the saving response to the gospel, the other is implied. Repentance often refers to our initial turning from sin, leading to salvation (Acts 11:18; 2 Tim 2:25). Ongoing repentance is a normal part of the Christian life and follows initial repentance. Ongoing repentance is turning from sins out of love for Jesus and a desire for God's glory. Repentance is a way of life, lasting until death, as we battle sin, yield to temptation, and repent to walk rightly. It involves spurning sinful thoughts, speech, and actions repeatedly (2 Cor 7:9; Rev 3:19). The idea of ongoing repentance often occurs in Scripture without the word *repent* or *repentance* being used (Rom 6:15–23; Heb 3:12–15; 1 John 1:8–10). *See also* application of salvation; conversion; faith.

responsibility—*See* faith; free will; Holy Spirit's gifts; Last Judgment.

rest, everlasting—*See* heaven.

restoration—*See* Christ's saving work, biblical images.

resurrection—God's bringing the physically dead back to life, raising their bodies from the grave. The resurrection of the body will occur at the end of the age (John 6:40), at Christ's return (1 Thess 4:16), before the Last Judgment and eternal state. God will raise all the dead (Dan 12:2; John 5:28–29; Acts 24:15). Evangelicals disagree as to how many stages will be involved in the resurrection. Amillennialism and postmillennialism hold to a one-stage general resurrection at the end of the age. Historic premillennialism asserts that the resurrection will occur in two stages. Before the millennium, God will raise deceased saints to take part in the thousand years. After the millennium, he will raise believers who died during the thousand years, along with all the unsaved. Dispensational premillennialism affirms three stages, adding a resurrection of church saints at the rapture. Scripture teaches that there will be continuity and discontinuity between our current bodies and our resurrection bodies but emphasizes continuity (Rom 8:11; Phil 3:21). Christ, the forerunner of resurrected human beings, was raised in his earthly body (John 2:19; 10:17–18). Since Jesus, the firstfruits of God's harvest, was raised in his earthly body, so will we be. There will also be discontinuity with our current bodies. Compare the "humble condition" of our bodies now with their future "likeness" to Christ's "glorious body" in the resurrection (Phil 3:20–21). Paul describes our current bodies as perishable, dishonored, weak, and mortal, and our resurrection bodies as imperishable, glorious, powerful, immortal, and spiritual (1 Cor 15:42–44, 53–54). Our present bodies are perishable, as we get sick, grow old, and die. They are dishonored, as they are put in the grave at death. They are weak, as even strong athletes learn in old age. They are mortal, not by creation but because of the fall, and eventually die. By contrast, our new bodies will be imperishable and immortal, incapable of getting sick or dying. They will be powerful and glorious. They will not grow tired or weak. Our bodies also will be "spiritual" (v. 44), not incorporeal but dominated by the Spirit and fitted for eternal life on the new earth. *See also* glorification; heaven; millennium; new heavens and new earth; preterism; Second Coming.

resurrection bodies—*See* glorification; resurrection.

resurrection of Christ—*See* Christ's saving work.

return of Christ—*See* Second Coming.

revelation—divine self-disclosure; God's graciously making himself known in general and special revelation. General (or natural) revelation is God's self-disclosure to all people always and everywhere, revealing who he is and making all accountable. In general revelation God reveals himself in creation (Ps 19:1–6; John 1:3–9; Rom 1:18–25), humanity (Eccl 3:11; Rom 1:32; 2:12–16), and history (Acts 14:14–18; 17:22–29). Special revelation is God's self-disclosure to specific people at particular times and places, enabling them to enter into salvation. The Bible distinguishes Old Testament and New Testament special revelation (Heb 1:1–2). Old Testament revelation includes theophanies, visions and dreams, the casting of lots, miracles, audible speech, and prophetic declaration. New Testament revelation includes all these varieties: theophanies (Acts 9:1–6), visions (10:9–16), dreams (Matt 1:20–21), the casting of lots (Acts 1:23–26), miracles (John 9:1–7), audible speech (12:27–29), prophetic declaration (Acts 2:14–36), the incarnation, and Scripture (John 14:25–26; 16:13–15; 2 Tim 3:14–17; 2 Pet 1:18–25; 3:16). New Testament revelation centers on the person and work of Christ. People are not saved through general revelation, for we actively suppress, distort, and misuse it. Jesus alone is Savior, and faith in Christ is the only means of receiving salvation. Although general revelation is insufficient for salvation, it is an important starting point for the gospel. As they urge unbelievers to turn to Christ in faith, missionaries do not start from scratch but build on the point of contact God has made with unbelievers in his general revelation. *See also* Christ's incarnation; mission; revelation, progressive; Scripture, attributes.

revelation, progressive—God's increasing revelation of himself as the biblical story moves along. Teachings unfold from Old Testament to New Testament, as Scripture itself notes (Heb 1:1–2). Therefore, we must understand the Old Testament in light of the fuller revelation of the New. And we must understand the New Testament in light of the previous revelation in the Old, as later revelation builds upon earlier revelation. Progressive revelation underlines the unity of the Bible and the development of God's revelation. Features of progressive revelation include Old Testament prophecy and types and New Testament fulfillment and anti-types. *See also* prophecy; revelation; type, typology.

rewards—*See* Last Judgment.

righteousness—(1) The virtue that humans produce, which falls short of God's standard for salvation: "There is no one righteous, not even one" (Rom 3:10). Only Christ's perfect righteousness pleases God. Paul explained his goal to "be found in him, not having a righteousness of [his] own from the law, but one that is through faith in Christ—the righteousness from God based on faith" (justification, Phil 3:9). (2) Moral uprightness that should describe Jesus's followers. God's people must be fair and unbiased in their decisions. They must "detest evil; [and] cling to what is good" (Rom 12:9). *See also* justice; justification; righteousness (justice) of God.

righteousness (justice) of God—God's moral order, by which he governs the world and treats all creatures justly. He cares for the poor and downtrodden. God is a just Judge, and, amazingly, his righteousness also brings salvation. God in wrath, an extension of his justice, hates sin. However, his relentless grace deals with his own wrath toward sinners to rescue them. Jesus saves us from God's wrath by dying as a propitiation to bear that wrath for us. In the future God will defeat evil, Satan, and all his foes. He and his people will win, the lost will suffer forever in hell, and God's justice will prevail (Ps 145:17; Acts 17:31; Rom 3:25; Jas 1:27; Rev 14:9–11). *See also* grace of God; justice; Last Judgment; wrath of God.

Roman Catholic church government—*See* church, government.

Roman Catholicism—one of the three major branches of Christianity, along with Eastern Orthodoxy and Protestantism. Eastern Orthodox churches split with the Roman Catholic Church in 1054, and Protestant churches split with it in the Reformation of the sixteenth century. Catholicism regards the pope as the infallible head of the church and supreme authority on earth. It holds to the dual authorities of tradition and Scripture rather than Protestantism's *sola scriptura*. It regards as a legal fiction Protestantism's view that in justification God declares sinners righteous, instead teaching that justification is a process in which the faithful grow in righteousness. Catholicism holds that God infuses grace to Christians through the sacraments, enabling them to merit eternal life. By contrast, Protestantism holds that God imputes Christ's righteousness to believers. *See also* baptism, views; Calvin, John; church, government; Eastern Orthodoxy; evangelicalism; Lord's Supper, views; Luther, Martin; Mary; Rahner, Karl; Reformation; Reformation *solas*; Teresa of Ávila.

Ss

Sabbath—a day of rest and worship. God commanded Israel to keep the seventh day as a holy day of rest, to follow his example (Gen 2:2–3; Exod 20:8–11) and to remember the exodus (Deut 5:12–15). Christians worship on Sunday, the Lord's Day, in remembrance of Jesus's resurrection (Acts 20:7). The Sabbath points toward the ultimate rest of heaven (Heb 4:9). *See also* heaven; Ten Commandments; worship.

Sabellianism—*See* Trinity.

sacerdotalism—*See* church, government.

sacrament—*See* ordinances or sacraments.

sacrifice of Christ—*See* Christ's saving work, biblical images.

salvation history—God's particular revelation of himself in the biblical stories of Old Testament Israel, Jesus, and the New Testament church. Salvation history is also called redemptive history or the history of redemption. Highlighting promise and fulfillment, God makes himself known as he fulfills his plan in Scripture's unfolding narrative of providence, salvation, and judgment. God is praised, for he "has made known his salvation. . . . He has remembered his steadfast love and faithfulness to the house of Israel. All the ends of the earth have seen the salvation of our God" (Ps 98:2–3 ESV). God gave Paul grace to preach Christ to the Gentiles. Paul's preaching illuminates "the mystery hidden for ages in God" the Creator and now revealed in his "multi-faceted wisdom . . . through the church" (Eph 3:8–10). All this "is according to his eternal purpose accomplished in Christ Jesus our Lord" (v. 11). *See also* prediction/fulfillment; providence.

sanctification—God's setting us apart from sin to himself, producing holiness in us now, and perfecting us in holiness at Christ's return. Holy God is the source of all holiness, and human holiness is not only separation from sin but also consecration to God. Sanctification occurs in union with Christ. When the Holy Spirit unites us to Christ, he frees us from sin's tyranny and, with our having been raised with Christ, empowers us to live new lives (Rom 6:1–4). The Trinity is active in our sanctification. The Father guides us through difficulties to "share his holiness" (Heb 12:10). The Son died on the cross to sanctify us (Eph 5:25–26). And the Holy Spirit also plays a role (2 Thess 2:13). God, the author of sanctification, enables us to be active participants (Phil 2:12–13; Col 1:28–29). Sanctification is past (definitive), present (progressive), and future (final). Definitive or past sanctification is the Spirit's work of setting us apart as holy to Christ, constituting us as saints. This occurred when we trusted Christ (1 Cor 1:2; 6:11). Present or progressive sanctification is the Spirit's work of enabling us to grow in applied holiness (1 Thess 4:3). Future or final sanctification is the Spirit's work of conforming us to Christ's image in perfect holiness at his return (Eph 5:27; 1 John 3:2). God sanctifies us as his people both individually (Heb 6:11–12) and corporately (10:24–25). Sanctification involves tensions, including knowing and doing; sanctification realized but not yet fully realized; and God's sovereignly sanctifying us and our being active, responsible agents. *See also* application of salvation; holiness; Holy Spirit's ministries; spiritual disciplines.

Sanneh, Lamin (1942–2019)—African missiologist and a convert from Islam to Christianity. Sanneh wrote on the relationship between Islam and Christianity and helped pioneer the study of world Christianity. He wrote many articles and a dozen books, including his memoir, *Summoned from the Margin: Homecoming of an African. See also* mission.

Satan and demons—fallen angels and their leader, originating in the rebellion of angels before the creation of humans. God created angels holy, but Satan and many others revolted against God and became fallen angels. Many think the prophets describe this rebellion, symbolized by the kings of Babylon and Tyre (Isa 14:12–14; Ezek 28:12–17). "The great dragon . . . the ancient serpent," or "the devil and Satan" (Rev 12:9), is an accuser (v. 10), deceiver (v. 9), liar, and murderer (John 8:44). Demons, also called unclean spirits (Matt 10:1), carry out Satan's evil plans by promoting idolatry (1 Cor

10:19–20) and false teaching (1 Tim 4:1) and sometimes possessing people (Matt 17:15, 18)—although not believers (1 John 4:4). Satan and demons hate God and believers and seek to devour them (1 Pet 5:8). Satan blinds unbelievers' minds to keep them from believing the gospel (2 Cor 4:4). The devil tempts believers to materialism (1 Tim 6:10), conceit (3:6), immorality (1 Cor 7:2, 5), lying (Acts 5:3), divisiveness (Titus 3:10–11), and false teaching (1 John 4:1–4). By God's strength, however, believers can resist the devil. God will punish Satan and demons eternally in hell (Matt 25:41). *See also* angels; Christ's saving work, biblical images; exorcism; Holy Spirit's works; idolatry.

satisfaction view—*See* Christ's saving work, historical views.

Savior—*See* Christ's names and titles.

Schleiermacher, Friedrich (1768–1834)—a German theologian, philosopher, and biblical scholar who tried to reconcile Enlightenment ideals with Protestantism. Rejecting orthodox Christianity, he is recognized as the father of liberalism. He lectured on theology and philosophy and influenced the development of higher criticism and hermeneutics. His most famous writing, *The Christian Faith* (1821–22) attempted to reform Protestant theology and brought him both renown and opposition from the theological schools. For him the fundamental principle of theology is not the Scriptures, the creeds, or rationalism, but the feeling of absolute dependence on God. *See also* Barth, Karl; evangelicalism; modernism; neoorthodoxy.

Scripture—the sixty-six books of the Bible, uniquely inspired by God. Scripture is the Word of God, the supreme authority for all faith and practice. *See also* canon; inspiration, views; Scripture, attributes; truth.

Scripture, attributes—qualities of the Bible as the Word of God, including necessity, clarity, sufficiency, and authority. The necessity of Scripture means that the Bible is necessary for salvation because it alone reveals the gospel (2 Tim 3:15–17). We need God's special revelation in his Word to learn the message of salvation, which is not revealed in the general revelation of creation or conscience. The clarity (or perspicuity) of Scripture means that God has produced Scripture so that people are able to understand its basic message (Ps 19:1–6). This does not mean that all things in it are equally easy to understand. It means instead that the gospel and the

Bible's basic teachings can be grasped. The sufficiency of Scripture means that God's Word provides all that we need to gain eternal life and to live lives pleasing to God (Luke 16:29–31; 2 Pet 1:3–4). This does not mean that we do not need anyone else. We need others to teach us, and they need us. The authority of Scripture means that because God gave the Word, it possesses his authority. By "authority" we mean the right to teach truth and command obedience (2 Tim 4:1–5). The Word of God is over us; we believe it and humbly obey it. *See also* inspiration, views; Scripture; truth.

seal—*See* Holy Spirit's names and descriptions.

second Adam—*See* Christ's humanity; Christ's saving work, biblical images.

"second blessing" theology—*See* Pentecostalism.

Second Coming—the return of Jesus Christ. It will be personal, visible, and glorious. Jesus's return will be personal: he himself will return, as he and his apostles foretell (Mark 13:26; Acts 1:11; Rev 22:20). He will come back to bless his own and judge the wicked (2 Thess 1:6–8). Jesus's return will be visible and unmistakable: he warns us not to be fooled by reports that Christ has returned secretly, because his coming will be very evident (Matt 24:23–27). John says that every eye will see the returning Christ (Rev 1:7). Jesus's return will also be glorious (Luke 21:27; Titus 2:13; 1 Pet 4:13), contrasting with his first humble advent (Phil 2:6–8). The second time he will come not to suffer and die but to judge and reign. Scripture says three things about the timing of the Second Coming. Some passages teach believers to look for Christ to come back (Mark 13:33–37; Heb 9:28; Rev 22:20). These texts emphasize readiness and love (2 Tim 4:8) for his return. Second, other passages teach that certain events will precede the Second Coming (Rom 11:25–26). Such texts stress patience as we consider the signs of the times. Third and most important, still other passages teach that no one knows when Jesus will return (Matt 25:13; Acts 1:6–7; 1 Thess 5:2–4). Such texts promote humility and wisdom, for we are ignorant of the timing of the Second Coming. The major purpose of the Second Coming texts is to promote spiritual preparedness, as Jesus's words indicate (Matt 24:44; Luke 21:36). *See also* "already" and "not yet"; preterism; signs of the times; tribulation.

second death—*See* death; hell.

seeing God—*See* heaven.

separation from God—*See* death; hell.

session of Christ—*See* Christ's saving work.

seven Spirits of God—*See* Holy Spirit's names and descriptions.

sign gifts—*See* charismatic gifts; Holy Spirit's gifts.

signs of the times—precursors of Christ's return that characterize the time between his advents. Jesus and the apostles foretell the coming of people or events that would anticipate his return. Since signs are characteristic of the whole period between the First and Second Coming, appearance of signs does not mean that the Second Coming will occur soon. Rather, each sign is both "already" and "not yet," fulfilled in part and awaiting greater fulfillment at Christ's return. His return will be unexpected by the careless and indifferent, as Peter warns (2 Pet 3:3–4). And it will be expected, although not predicted, by the watchful (2 Tim 4:8). Some signs show God's grace. Chief among them is Jesus's prediction of the preaching of the gospel to the nations (Matt 24:14). Other signs show opposition to God. These include tribulation, apostasy, and antichrists, including the Antichrist. Following Daniel, Jesus predicts that God will visit the earth with terrible wrath because of human rebellion, referring to both the destruction of Jerusalem in AD 70 and the future great tribulation (Dan 12:1; Matt 24:21–22). Jesus and Paul warn of another sign of opposition to God: apostasy, the renouncing of a faith once professed (Matt 24:10; 2 Thess 2:1–3). Antichrists are people who deny that Jesus is God's Messiah (1 John 2:22); *the* Antichrist is the final pseudo-messiah. John speaks of both (1 John 2:18, 22; see also Paul's warning in 2 Thess 2:3–10). Still other signs show God's judgment. Jesus told of signs displaying God's judgment of obstinate people. These include wars and natural phenomena, such as famines and earthquakes (Matt 24:6–7). *See also* "already" and "not yet;" antichrist(s); Second Coming; tribulation.

simplicity of God—*See* unity of God.

simul justus et peccator—*See* justification.

sin—any disobedience to God's law. There is a key distinction between original sin and actual sin. Original sin is the result of the primal sin of Adam and Eve for humans. God made our first parents sinless and in fellowship with him. Nevertheless, they rebelled against their Maker, sinned, and brought God's curse into the world. Adam's first sin is the cause of sin and death entering the world of humans. There are various views of original sin. Pelagianism (named for the Irish monk Pelagius) erred and held that Adam was merely a bad example that others follow. Augustine (and Augustinianism) opposed Pelagius, insisting that Adam's sin plunged the human race into sin. Headship views say that Adam's standing for his race is the cause of humans' inheriting sin's guilt (condemnation before God) and corruption (moral defilement). Natural headship (or realism) holds that we really were in Adam in seed form; thus, his sin is ours. Federal headship holds that Adam was our representative, and his sin is counted (imputed) to our spiritual bank accounts (Genesis 3; Rom 5:12–19; Eph 2:1–3). Actual sins are the acts of sin that humans commit. It is noteworthy that before Paul treats original sin in Rom 5:12–19, he deals with actual sins in 1:18–3:20 (cf. Gen 6:5; Gal 5:19–21). *See also* conscience; fall, the; guilt; indwelling sin; sin nature; theodicy; unpardonable sin.

sin nature—since the fall, the natural tendency to sin present in all humans from birth. It remains in believers, although God regenerates them, and gives them his Spirit, who leads them in holiness. *See also* indwelling sin; sin.

singing—*See* worship.

sinlessness of Christ—*See* Christ's incarnation; Christ's saving work.

skepticism (or scepticism)—the philosophical view that sure knowledge is impossible. Skepticism thus doubts any claims of knowledge, including religious knowledge. *See also* agnosticism; apatheism; atheism; dualism; idealism; materialism; monism; naturalism; revelation; truth; truthfulness of God.

social gospel—an early twentieth-century movement of labor reforms led by liberal Protestant ministers, including Walter Rauschenbusch and Washington Gladden.

social justice—*See* poor, the.

sola scriptura—the Bible alone as the paramount source of all theology. We employ other sources—including reason, tradition, and experience— but deliberately and consistently subordinate them to Scripture. These other sources help us interpret Scripture and must be judged by Scripture, the highest standard. *See also* Reformation *solas*; Scripture; Scripture, attributes.

Son of God—*See* Christ's deity; Christ's names and titles; Trinity.

Son of Man—*See* Christ's humanity; Christ's names and titles.

soteriology—in Christian theology, the study of the doctrine of salvation, including election, union with Christ, and the application of salvation (calling, regeneration, faith, justification, adoption, sanctification, perseverance, and glorification).

soul—*See* humanity, makeup.

soul sleep—*See* intermediate state.

sovereignty of God—God's supreme authority and rule over all. He plans and guides all things to his goals. God governs nature and the history of nations and ordains our lives. His sovereign plan is never foiled. God is sovereign and humans are responsible, though putting these truths together is beyond our understanding. God's reign means that ultimately he wins, evil loses, and justice prevails (Ps 33:10–11; 103:19; 139:16; 1 Tim 6:15). *See also* Arminianism; Arminius, James; Calvin, John; compatibilism; foreordination; incompatibilism; providence; Reformation; will of God.

speaking in tongues—In Acts 2:4, when the Holy Spirit filled the apostles, they "began to speak in different tongues," languages they did not know, which their hearers understood (v. 11). In 1 Cor 12 and 14, Paul uses the same terminology to refer to a spiritual gift being used in the Corinthian church that needs interpretation. Christians debate whether Paul refers to the unknown languages of Acts 2 or to unintelligible speech. Ecstatic speech is a widespread feature of Pentecostal worship around the world today. *See also* charismatic gifts; Holy Spirit's gifts; Pentecostalism.

special revelation—*See* revelation.

spirit—*See* humanity, makeup.

Spirit of Christ—*See* Holy Spirit's names and descriptions.

Spirit of the Father—*See* Holy Spirit's names and descriptions.

Spirit of the Son—*See* Holy Spirit's names and descriptions.

spiritual body—*See* resurrection.

spiritual death—*See* death; hell.

spiritual disciplines—scriptural practices that promote believers' spiritual maturity. God desires us to cultivate habits of devotion, time-honored activities of Bible reading and meditation (Ps 1:2), prayer (Phil 4:6), worship (Eph 5:18–20), witnessing (Matt 28:19–20), and fellowship (Heb 10:24–25). Spiritual growth requires self-control (Gal 5:23) and discipline (1 Tim 4:7). The spiritual disciplines are taught or modeled in God's Word; therefore, reading, hearing, meditating on, memorizing, and studying the Word are primary. Prayer too is vital for our spiritual growth. We offer prayers of praise, thanks, confession, intercession, and petition with commitment and concentration. Although believers engage in some spiritual disciplines alone, God uses the church to help us grow. The disciplines are means, not ends, and point to God's glory. *See also* confession (1); prayer; sanctification; Scripture; virtues, Christian; worship.

spiritual gifts—*See* Holy Spirit's gifts.

spirituality—growing in a relationship with God through Jesus Christ in the Spirit. Involves believers' spiritual formation in the church, with a goal of likeness to Christ by walking with God based on the truths of his Word, which are lived out for his glory and by his power (Rom 12:1–2; 1 Corinthians 13; Gal 5:16–26). By contrast, the world has much interest in general "spirituality." This is an interest in things of the human spirit or soul over against material things. This spirituality involves subjective "sacred" experiences often without involvement in organized religion. *See also* Holy Spirit's works; prayer; sanctification; Scripture; worship.

spirituality of God—God as a spiritual Being, without a human body. Although the Bible speaks of God's eyes, ears, and hands, he does not have bodily members. Rather, such expressions are anthropomorphisms that speak of God as if he were a human being. When Scripture speaks of God as having a physical presence, it means that he, an invisible Spirit, reveals himself physically (Deut 4:15–19; Isa 6:1–4; John 1:18; 4:24; 1 Tim 1:17; 1 John 4:11–12). *See also* anthropomorphism; anthropopathism; attributes of God.

sprinkling, baptism by—*See* baptism, mode.

Spurgeon, Charles Haddon (1834–1892)—English Baptist preacher, still influential among many Christians; pastor of the Metropolitan Tabernacle in London for thirty-eight years. Defended the 1689 London Baptist Confession of Faith and opposed the liberal theologies of his day. Author of many works but most remembered for powerful sermons of biblical exposition and penetrating application. *See also* liberalism; preaching.

stewardship—a God-given responsibility, involving authority and accountability.

subordinationism—the subservience of the Son to the Father. (1) Ontological subordinationism: the Son is eternally subservient to the Father and thus is not God (a heresy); (2) Functional (or economic) subordinationism: the Son becomes subservient to the Father in the incarnation and state of humiliation (John 14:28; 17:4). *See also*: Christ's deity; Christ's deity, denials; Christ's incarnation; Christ's states of humiliation and exaltation.

substantive view of image—*See* image of God (*imago Dei*).

substitution—Christ's atoning death in the place of sinners. We cannot save ourselves from our sin and its ultimate consequence, but in love Christ (our federal head) gives himself to die for us so that we might receive forgiveness and eternal life (Isa 53:5; Gal 3:13; 1 Pet 3:18). *See also* Christ's saving work, biblical images; Christ's saving work, historical views; propitiation.

suffering—enduring bodily, mental, or emotional pain or distress. God is good and did not create suffering or evil. He created a good world for the good of humans made in his image. The fall brought sin, suffering, and death as intruders into the world for Adam and Eve and all their descendants. Sadly, suffering characterizes human existence since the fall. In mercy, the Creator became a creature: the Son of God became a man, even the Suffering Servant. His suffering and death save believers forever, drive the Christian life, and guarantee our future glory. Jesus tells believers to expect suffering (John 16:33), which God uses to build endurance, character, and hope (Rom 5:3–4; Jas 1:2–4). When Jesus returns, God will triumph, judge justly, and reign forever. Suffering will end for all of God's people, as God will perfect us in his image and give us true freedom, incomparable glory, and joy. *See also* Christ's saving work; fall, the; hell; persecution; sin.

Suffering Servant—*See* Christ's names and titles; Christ's saving work, biblical images.

sufficiency of Scripture—*See* Scripture; Scripture, attributes.

syncretism—the combining of diverse religious beliefs and practices. When this occurs, the result is often a new religious system. When Old Testament Israel sought to fuse the worship of Yahweh with that of Baal, God's anger burned against his wayward people (Hos 2:2–13). Although believers must contextualize the gospel so people in the world's diverse cultures can understand and believe it, believers must be on guard against syncretism. The danger is that the gospel can be compromised by the mixing of teachings and practices that cannot be reconciled with biblical Christianity. *See also* contextualization; exclusivism/inclusivism/pluralism; greatness of God; idolatry.

synergism—*See* monergism/synergism.

systematic theology—the integrating and synthesizing of doctrinal conclusions based on exegetical, biblical, and historical theology. Systematics seeks to incorporate primary biblical themes, address central theological topics, and show interrelationships between doctrines. *See also* biblical theology; doctrine; exegesis; historical theology; practical theology; theological method.

Tt

temple of the Spirit—*See* church, pictures.

temptation—solicitation to do evil from one of three sources: the world, the flesh, or the devil. "The world" here refers not to God's beautiful creation that he will redeem in the new earth but to the sinful world system set against God and his people (Eph 2:1–31; 1 John 2:15–17). The world tempts us with fame, fortune, and lust. "The flesh" here is not the human body as God's creation that he will raise on the last day but rather humans' sinful, innate tendency to rebel ever since the fall. Our flesh is easily enticed to desire contrary to God's will (Jas 1:14–15). The devil, who hates God and believers, works to keep people from coming to faith and seeks to destroy Christians (2 Cor 4:4; 1 Pet 5:8–9). We thank God that he is stronger than all our foes, has defeated them in Christ's death and resurrection, and will sanctify us completely when Jesus returns victoriously. *See also* Christ's saving work, images; indwelling sin; sanctification; Satan and demons; Second Coming; sin.

Ten Commandments—the Ten Words that form the core of the law that God gave Israel through Moses at Mount Sinai (Exod 20:1–17; Deut 5:6–21). They reveal the will of God, the Lawgiver. They deal with monotheism, idolatry, God's name, the Sabbath, honoring parents, murder, adultery, stealing, giving false testimony, and coveting. Obedience to the law was not the people's way to salvation. Rather, God commanded them to obey the law as their loving response to him for redeeming them from Egyptian bondage (Exod 20:2, 6). He desired them to reflect him and serve him as his kingdom of priests and a holy nation (Exod 19:4–6). The Commandments are also a powerful tool to show sinners their need for salvation (Rom 7:7–13;

Gal 3:24). Christ kept the law perfectly and died to pay the legal debt that his people could not pay. Jesus summarized the law (and the Prophets) as love for God and neighbor (Matt 22:37–40). As a result, the law is an important guide for the Christian life (Gal 5:14; Jas 2:8, 12). *See also* antinomianism; asceticism; idolatry; law, uses; legalism; sanctification.

Teresa of Ávila (1515–1582)—a Spanish Carmelite nun, known for her spiritual mysticism. After entering the Carmelite convent of the Incarnation in Ávila (c. 1535), she became very ill. During this illness, she testified to having an ecstatic experience by reading mystics. Chagrined at the laxity of the religious life, she founded a convent in 1562 to restore the Carmelites to their original poverty and austerity. She founded and nurtured sixteen more convents in Spain. Teresa was canonized a saint in 1622 and, in 1970, became the first woman to be declared a Doctor of the Roman Catholic Church. She penned spiritual classics, including *The Way of Perfection* (1583) and *The Interior Castle* (1588). *See also* mysticism; Roman Catholicism.

Tertullian (c. 160–220)—a major early Christian theologian whose Latin shaped the vocabulary and thought of Western Christianity. He wrote against heresy and in defense of the faith on many theological topics, including the resurrection, baptism, the doctrine of humanity, original sin, and faith and reason. He addressed many practical issues, including prayer, appropriate dress, military service, fleeing persecution, marriage, and the theater. Late in life, Tertullian joined a prophetic sectarian movement called Montanism because many Christians lacked moral rigor. He coined the term *Trinity* and taught that God was one substance in three persons. *See also* baptism; persecution; resurrection; sin; Trinity.

thanksgiving—*See* prayer.

theistic evolution—*See* humanity, origin.

theodicy—an attempt to explain why God allows evil in the world. This is a subset of the larger problem of evil. A theodicy attempts to vindicate God's omnipotence, goodness, justice, and providence in light of the existence of evil and suffering in the world. *See also* apologetics; fall, the; problem of evil; sin.

theological interpretation of Scripture—reading the Bible while taking into account its theological character and theology's influence on interpreters. The theological interpretation of Scripture emphasizes the inspired biblical text, its message (the history of salvation), and readers' theological concerns. It takes a high view of Scripture, which it reads to learn of God's story. *See also* hermeneutics; inspiration; inspiration, views.

theological method—the process used to formulate a systematic theology. There have been various methods, including those that emphasize tradition (as books on the theology of Karl Barth), reason (as Paul Tillich's correlation of existentialism with Christian theology), and experience (as in Jürgen Moltmann's thought). For evangelical theology, Scripture is paramount. The foundation of a sound method is exegesis, understanding the meaning of biblical passages. Next comes biblical theology, placing biblical texts into God's unfolding plan that moves from creation and the fall to redemption and new creation. It is important not to read the Bible individualistically but to consider historical theology. Work in biblical exegesis, biblical theology, and history points toward a theological synthesis. And theology is incomplete without practical theology, the living out of biblical truth in the church. *See also* biblical theology; doctrine; exegesis; historical theology; practical theology; systematic theology.

theology—the study of God. Strictly, theology is the doctrine of God, also called theology proper. More generally, theology includes the study of knowing God, his revelation, the Trinity, God's attributes and works, humanity and sin, Jesus and his saving work, the Holy Spirit and salvation, the church, the future, and the Christian life. *See also* biblical theology; doctrine; historical theology; practical theology; systematic theology; theological method.

theology of hope—*See* Moltmann, Jürgen.

theology proper—in Christian theology, the study of the doctrine of God, including the Trinity, God's attributes, and works. *See also* attributes of God; Trinity; works of God.

theology, sources—means of acquiring data in order to construct a valid theology. Four sources of theology are time-honored: Scripture, reason, tradition, and experience. Scripture is the principal source that sits in judgment of the other sources. Our reason reflects on revelation each time we do theology. Reason clarifies concepts, enables us to reject false dichotomies, see truths in relationships, and analyzes systems. Tradition offers us the wisdom of our predecessors. It conveys the church's teachings (in creeds and confessions), corrects errors, and offers historical perspectives on doctrinal issues. We use experience in doing theology. Experience helps us as whole persons interpret Scripture's teaching through the lens of our backgrounds, cultures, life situations, faith experiences, and church life. We all use tradition, reason, and experience in studying theology. They are good but fallible guides, and we must judge each by Scripture, the only ultimate source (*sola scriptura*). *See also* confession (3); Scripture; *sola scriptura*; truth.

theophany—a visible appearance of God to humans, especially in the Old Testament. Examples include God's appearances to Abraham (Gen 17:1) and Moses (Exod 3:1–6). These are to be distinguished from Old Testament appearances of Christ (Christophanies). Theophanies are also to be distinguished from the incarnation because they were temporary, whereas the incarnation is permanent. Christ is the God-man forevermore. *See also* Christophany; Christ's incarnation.

tongues—*See* charismatic gifts; Holy Spirit's gifts; Pentecostalism; speaking in tongues.

total depravity—sin's effect on all aspects of human nature so that we cannot earn God's favor. This misunderstood term does not mean that human beings are as sinful as they could be or that unsaved people can do no good. Rather, it means that since the fall, sin pervades humans and every aspect of their lives, including their minds, wills, attitudes, words, actions, and ways (Rom 3:9–20). Paul especially underscores the effects of sin on the human mind (Rom 1:21–22; Eph 4:17; Col 1:21). We each have an inner, ongoing propensity to sin, as Jesus taught (Mark 7:20–23). The most significant consequence of total depravity is that we are unable to save ourselves from sin (Matt 19:24–26; 1 Cor 2:14; 2 Cor 4:3–4). *See also* death; grace of God; guilt; indwelling sin; sin.

tradition—*See* theology, sources.

transcendence of God—*See* omnipresence of God.

transubstantiation—*See* Aquinas, Thomas; Lord's Supper, views; Roman Catholicism.

tribulation—in Scripture (1) the general hardship and distress that God's people must endure (John 16:33 ESV; Acts 14:22 ESV; Rom 12:12 ESV); (2) the great tribulation: intense, global suffering preceding the Second Coming (Matt 24:21 ESV). Some teach that the church will be spared the great tribulation. Others teach that the church will endure it protected by God's power. *See also* dispensationalism; millennium; rapture; Second Coming; signs of the times.

trichotomy—*See* humanity, makeup.

trinitarian heresies—*See* Trinity.

Trinity—almighty God's eternal existence in three persons: Father, Son, and Holy Spirit. The Father is the First Person of the Trinity, the Son the Second Person, and the Spirit the Third Person. These three persons are one God and are inseparable, sharing the same essence. We distinguish the persons from one another but do not confuse them. We thus hold that only the Son of God became a man and died for our sins. Each person is fully God, and mysteriously, the three divine persons indwell one another (this is called *perichoresis*). Although in unity they share all of their works, they perform specific tasks. To cite an example, Scripture attributes the source of redemption to the Father (in election), its accomplishment to the Son (in his death and resurrection), and its application to the Spirit (in regeneration and conversion). Biblical underpinning for the Trinity includes Deut 6:4; Matt 3:16–17; John 14:10–11; 2 Cor 13:13; 1 Tim

2:5; and 1 Pet 1:1–2. Heresies that rejected the Trinity included Modalistic and Dynamic Monarchianism, both of which emphasized the unity of God. Modalistic Monarchianism (modalism or Sabellianism) held that the three persons were divine successively, not simultaneously. The one God revealed himself first as Father, then as Son, and finally as Holy Spirit. Dynamic Monarchianism (or adoptionism) denied the deity of the Son, holding instead that God "adopted" him at his baptism. *See also* Christ's deity; Christ's deity, denials; Holy Spirit's deity; Trinity, ontological/economic.

Trinity, ontological/economic—the distinction between (1) the eternal relationships between the three persons of the one God and (2) their relationships to the world. The ontological (or immanent) Trinity concerns the eternal distinctions in the relationships of the Father, Son, and Holy Spirit apart from their works of creation and salvation. The personal characteristics that distinguish the persons are these: "It is proper to the Father to beget the Son, and to the Son to be begotten of the Father, and to the Holy Ghost to proceed from the Father and the Son from all eternity" (Westminster Larger Catechism 10). The economic Trinity concerns the roles that the Father, Son, and Holy Spirit play in creation, and especially in salvation. The Father sends the Son to rescue the lost, the Son performs the work of redemption, and the Spirit applies salvation to believers. *See also* Christ's deity; Holy Spirit's deity; Trinity.

true freedom—*See* free will.

true vine—*See* Christ's names and titles.

truth—that which is in agreement with fact or reality. The biblical concept of truth involves faithfulness, factualness, and completeness. Because the Father (Isa 45:19; John 3:33; Titus 1:2), Son (John 8:40; 14:6; 18:37), and Holy Spirit (John 14:17; 15:26; 16:13) are the truth and speak only the truth, Scripture is true in all three senses. Faithfulness: God faithfully reveals himself and his will in his Word (Ps 145:13; Rev 21:5). Factualness: Scripture corresponds to factual and spiritual reality (Ps 119:160; John 17:17; 2 Tim 2:15). Completeness: In Scripture God provides all we need for eternal life and godliness (Luke 16:29–31; 2 Pet 1:3–4). *See also* doctrine; heresy; systematic theology; truthfulness of God.

truthfulness of God—God's identity as the only true God and as one who always speaks the truth. Both Testaments affirm that there is only one living and true God. The true God always speaks the truth and never lies. Therefore, he and his Word are true and trustworthy (1 Sam 15:29; Jer 10:10; John 17:17; Titus 1:2). *See also* aseity of God; idolatry; Ten Commandments; truth; unity of God.

two ages—the age in which we live and the coming one. The New Testament contrasts two ages, "this [present] age" and "that age" or "the one to come" (Eph 1:21). This current age is characterized by evil (Gal 1:4), spiritual blindness (2 Cor 4:4), and spiritual death (Eph 2:1–2). The age to come is characterized by "the resurrection from the dead" (Luke 20:35–36), "eternal life" (Luke 18:30), and amazing displays of God's grace (Eph 2:7). In one sense, the consummation of the ages has come, for this present age is the fulfillment of the Old Testament hope (1 Cor 10:11; Heb 1:1–2; 9:26), but greater things await in the coming age. In this age believers experience a foretaste of the age to come (Heb 6:4–6). *See also* "already" and "not yet"; Second Coming.

Tyndale, William (c.1494–c.1536)—English scholar and key Reformation figure who translated the Bible into English from Hebrew and Greek. He famously said, "I will cause a boy who drives the plow to know more of the Scripture than the pope." In 1536 he was condemned and executed for translating the Bible into English. The Tyndale Bible played an ongoing role in spreading Reformation ideas and significantly influenced the King James Bible of 1611. *See also* Reformation.

type, typology—Old Testament persons, events, or institutions that prefigure Christ and the new covenant, the study of which is typology. New Testament fulfillments of Old Testament types are called antitypes. Adam (Rom 5:18–19; 1 Cor 15:22, 45) and Melchizedek (Hebrews 7) were types of Christ, the second Adam and king-priest. The exodus from Egyptian bondage and Passover were types of Christ's deliverance of believers from sin (Luke 9:31, where the Greek word for "departure" is *exodus*;

1 Cor 5:7; 1 Pet 1:18–19). The institutions of prophet (Heb 1:1–2), priest (v. 3), and king (v. 8) foretold Jesus, who would occupy all three offices. Although sometimes confused with allegory, typology is very different because it is rooted in history. Old Testament types are people, occurrences, and institutions that play important roles in the history of Israel. At the same time, they predict in action the coming Redeemer. Types thus demonstrate the unity of Scripture. *See also* Christ's offices; hermeneutics; revelation, progressive.

Uu

unchangeableness of God—*See* immutability of God.

unconditional election—*See* Calvinism; election.

union with Christ—the Holy Spirit's work of joining all believers to Christ so that all his saving benefits become ours. Also called mystical union. The Father plans salvation, the Son accomplishes it, and the Spirit applies it. What Christ has done for us is applied to us through union with him. Union with Christ is necessary because we were separated from him and salvation (Eph 2:12). By God's grace we participate in many aspects of Jesus's story. Union with Jesus's death and resurrection empowers believers for progressive sanctification (Rom 6:4). Through union we sit spiritually with him in heaven (Eph 2:6). We receive all of salvation's blessings "in Christ," including regeneration, justification, adoption, sanctification, perseverance, resurrection, and glorification. Because of union, we belong to Jesus and he belongs to us, and thus Christians enjoy an intimate spiritual relationship with him (1 Cor 6:17). Union will last forever, for the Father seals us in union with Christ with the Spirit "for the day of redemption" (Eph 4:30). Even death does not separate us from Christ, for we die in union with him (Rev 14:13). *See also* application of salvation; Lord's Supper.

unity of God—the attribute of God as one. Scripture teaches monotheism, that there is only one living and true God. God is one and is not composed of parts (this is known as God's simplicity). We distinguish his attributes but do not separate them (Deut 6:4–5; 1 Tim 2:5–6; Jas 2:14–26). *See also* attributes of God.

169

unity of the church—*See* church, attributes.

universalism—the view that, in the end, all human beings will be gathered into the love of God and be saved. Universalists claim that a loving God would never allow anyone to suffer forever in hell. They teach that if there is a hell, it is a place of purification, preparing souls for ultimate salvation. Most universalists reject Jesus's deity, miracles, and substitutionary atonement and hold instead that he died merely to demonstrate God's love. Universalists joined Unitarians in 1961 to form the Unitarian Universalist Association. Today, universalists seek closer relationships with non-Christian religions. Universalism is a major error, strongly opposed by Scripture (Matt 25:41, 46; Mark 9:43–48; 2 Thess 1:9–10; Rev 20:14–15; 21:8). *See also* heaven; hell; love of God; Origen.

universality of the church—*See* church, attributes.

unpardonable sin—the sin described by Jesus's assertion that "whoever blasphemes against the Holy Spirit never has forgiveness, but is guilty of an eternal sin" (Mark 3:29). According to various views, Jesus refers to denial of the faith, unbelief until death, or heinous sin, like murder or adultery. Apostasy is a great sin; although apostates sometimes repent, many do not, showing that their faith was not genuine. Not trusting Christ and dying in sin is *unforgiven* sin, but that differs from committing the *unpardonable* sin while still alive. Murder and adultery are wicked, but Scripture gives examples of offenders who were forgiven, such as David. The context of Jesus's statement suggests a better view. Immediately before Jesus's words, his enemies attributed his miracles done in the power of the Holy Spirit to Satan. This is the unpardonable sin: deliberately attributing Jesus's work to the devil. Those who fear they have committed the unpardonable sin have not done so; for if they had, they would not seek pardon. *See also* apostasy; Satan and demons; sin.

Vatican I (1869–1870)—the twentieth ecumenical council of the Roman Catholic Church convened in Rome by Pope Pius IX. It dealt with matters of faith and reason and condemned theological liberalism, rationalism, pantheism, and materialism. It is best known for defining as dogma (official teaching) the authority of the pope—the claims that he has supreme jurisdiction over the church, supreme teaching power, and infallibility, being free from error when he definitively teaches a doctrine. *See also* Roman Catholicism; Vatican II.

Vatican II (1962–1965)—the twenty-first ecumenical council of the Roman Catholic Church convened in Rome by Pope John XXIII and closed by Pope Paul VI. It updated the Church in the modern world. It treated the relation of the Catholic Church to other Christians and other world religions. It allowed vernacular languages to be used in the liturgy of the mass. It reaffirmed the Church's commitment to tradition and Scripture and expressed an open attitude to the scholarly study of Scripture. *See also* Rahner, Karl; Roman Catholicism; Vatican I.

verbal inspiration—*See* inspiration; inspiration, views.

vices—*See* sin; virtues, Christian.

victory—*See* Christ's saving work, biblical images; Christ's saving work, historical views; Second Coming.

virgin birth—*See* Christ's incarnation; Christ's saving work.

virtues, Christian—positive moral and spiritual character qualities that God builds into his saved people. The New Testament contains lists of virtues (Eph 4:32; Phil 4:8; 1 Tim 6:11; Jas 3:17; 1 Pet 3:8). God's grace in salvation is the source of the virtues believers are to cultivate by the Spirit. The greatest virtue is love (1 Cor 13:13), which has a prominent place on virtue lists. Combining virtues from three key New Testament virtue lists, while eliminating repetition, yields: "joy, peace, patience, kindness, goodness, faithfulness, gentleness, and self-control" (Gal 5:22–23); "compassion," "humility," longsuffering, gratitude (Col 3:12–15); "endurance," "godliness," and "brotherly affection" (2 Pet 1:6–7). The virtues are summarized in Christlikeness, which involves following Jesus's example by the power of the Spirit. For this reason, Scripture also calls them "the fruit of the Spirit" (Gal 5:22–23). Vices, negative moral character qualities, are the opposite of Christian virtues and also appear in New Testament lists (Mark 7:21–22; Gal 5:19–21; Col 3:5, 8; 2 Tim 3:2–5; 1 Pet 4:3). *See also* Holy Spirit's ministries; sanctification; spiritual disciplines.

visible church—*See* church.

vision of God—*See* heaven.

walking in the Spirit—*See* Holy Spirit's ministries.

weeping and gnashing of teeth—*See* hell.

Wesley, John (1703–1791)—English minister and theologian who, with his brother Charles and friend George Whitefield, founded Methodism. After an evangelical conversion, though facing opposition, Wesley traveled and preached the gospel outdoors. His ministry spanned many years and covered thousands of miles on horseback as he promoted the evangelical revival of Great Britain and beyond. He organized small Christian discipleship groups that stressed accountability and appointed itinerant evangelists to do the same. Doctrinal distinctives included Arminianism, prevenient grace, and Christian perfectionism. Wesley also inspired the Holiness movement and Pentecostalism. *See also* Arminianism; Arminius, James; Great Commission; Methodists; perfectionism; preaching; prevenient grace; Wesley, Susanna; Wesleyanism.

Wesley, Susanna (1669–1742)—a faithful woman who endured much hardship to raise two sons who changed the world. Wesley was well acquainted with adversity. She was the mother of nineteen children, nine of whom died at birth. She was married to Samuel, a sometimes difficult pastor with little business sense. She managed a large household and educated her children. Wesley spent time at night with every child once a week. Two of these were John and Charles, whom God used to bring gospel revival to Great Britain and beyond. *See also* Methodists; Wesley, John.

Wesleyanism—the theology and churches associated with John Wesley, founder of Methodism. Arminian in orientation, Wesleyans emphasize prevenient grace—grace that gives all individuals opportunity to believe the gospel—and entire sanctification or Christian perfection, the view that believers may love God so totally in this life as to be freed from sin. *See also* Arminianism; Arminius, James; perfectionism; prevenient grace; Wesley, John.

Westminster Confession of Faith—a statement of faith completed by an assembly of 151 Presbyterian and Puritan theologians at Westminster Abbey in 1646 in an effort to reform Anglicanism. It remains the standard of doctrine for many Presbyterian churches throughout the world and was adapted by some Baptists and Congregationalists as a basis for their doctrinal statements. The Westminster Confession, considered subordinate to the Bible, is a systematic exposition of Calvinism, written from a Puritan viewpoint. The assembly also produced the Westminster Larger and Shorter Catechisms as teaching instruments. *See also* Calvin, John; Calvinism; confession (3); Puritanism; Reformation.

will of God—(1) God's sovereign will, whereby he ordains all things that happen (Acts 4:27–28); (2) God's revealed will, whereby he commands obedience (Matt 28:19–20); (3) God's disposition of what pleases or displeases him (1 Tim 2:4). *See also* obedience; sovereignty of God.

wisdom of God—God's application of his knowledge in order to accomplish his goals. Both Testaments extol him whose great wisdom is unsearchable and unquestionable. God displays his wisdom in all his works, especially creation and redemption. He generously gives wisdom to those who ask in faith (Job 12:13; Rom 11:33; Jas 1:5). *See also* omniscience of God.

witness of the Spirit—*See* assurance of salvation; Holy Spirit's ministries.

Word of God—(1) Jesus as God's self-revelation; (2) the gospel preached; (3) the Scriptures. In the Old Testament, the Word of God is especially his speaking through the prophets (e.g., Jer 1:1–3). In the New Testament, the eternal Son of God, "the Word [who] was God," became a man. "The Word became flesh" (John 1:1, 14) and revealed God as never before (v. 18). The good news preached is also the Word of God: "When you received the word of God that you heard from us, you welcomed it not as a human message, but as it truly is, the word of God, which also works effectively in you who believe" (1 Thess 2:13; see also 1 Pet 1:23–25). The apostles' preaching is the Word of God, and so is their writing. In fulfillment of Jesus's words, they produced the New Testament, which, along with the Old Testament, is our God-given norm for faith and life (2 Tim 2:15; Heb 4:12). *See also* Chicago Statement on Biblical Inerrancy; inerrancy; revelation; Scripture; Scripture, attributes; *sola scriptura*.

work of Christ—*See* Christ's saving work; Christ's saving work, biblical images; Christ's saving work, historical views.

works of God—that which God does (in contrast to his attributes, which are the characteristics that make him God). These include creation, providence, redemption, and consummation. *See also* Christ's saving work; creation; Holy Spirit's works; providence; Second Coming.

world, the—*See* creation; temptation.

worship—private or public offering of adoration and praise to God according to his will. Individual believers set aside special times to express their love and thanks to God while also honoring him through faithful and obedient living. Corporate new covenant worship occurs when the church, "a people for his possession," gathers to "proclaim the praises of the one who called" it "out of darkness into his marvelous light" (1 Pet 2:9). Public worship involves pastors giving "attention to public reading, exhortation, and teaching" of Scripture and preaching "the word" so as to "rebuke, correct, and encourage with great patience and teaching" (1 Tim 4:13; 2 Tim 4:2). It includes letting "the word of Christ dwell richly among" us through the Spirit, "in all wisdom teaching and admonishing one another through psalms, hymns, and spiritual songs, singing to God with gratitude in" our "hearts" (Col 3:16). It involves praying always "in the Spirit with every prayer and request, staying alert with all perseverance and intercession for all the saints" (Eph 6:18). Worship also involves faithful practice of the ordinances Jesus gave the church: baptism and the Lord's Supper. *See also* liturgy; ordinances or sacraments; prayer; preaching; Sabbath.

wrath of God—God's personal, active, and settled anger toward sin, as an extension of his holiness and justice. Even in the midst of many biblical demonstrations of God's wrath, his grace relentlessly shines through. Astoundingly, Jesus voluntarily dies as a propitiation to save us from God's wrath by bearing that wrath for us. God presently reveals his wrath against rebellion, but the full demonstration of his wrath is still future. The coming wrath is both tragic and good. Jesus weeps over Jerusalem's unbelief and coming judgment. But judgment and hell also represent God's victory over evil and Satan, and all his foes, when God will avenge his people (Matt 23:37–39; Rom 3:25–26; 2 Thess 1:5–9; Rev 14:9–11). *See also* fear of God; hell; holiness of God; propitiation.

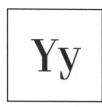

Yahweh—*See* God, names of.

young earth creationism—*See* humanity, origin.

Zz

Zwingli, Ulrich (1484–1531)—leader of the Swiss Protestant Reformation who held to the supreme authority of the Scriptures, which he rigorously applied to all doctrines and practices. His biblical study as an ordained Catholic priest moved him to critique first the practices and later the teaching of the Roman Catholic Church. He participated in disputations, public debates, that led some Swiss cantons to decide for the Reformation. He founded schools, including a seminary to train Reformed pastors. Both his preaching and writing sparked reformation, including his *Commentary on True and False Religion* (1525). Zwingli clashed with Luther over the Lord's Supper. They both rejected the mass as a sacrifice and transubstantiation, but Luther held to a real presence of Christ in, with, and under the bread and wine, while Zwingli held to a more symbolic view. *See also* Calvin, John; Lord's Supper, views; Luther, Martin; Reformation; Reformation *solas*.

Zwinglian view of the Lord's Supper—*See* Lord's Supper, views.